MASTERMINDS Riddle Math *Series*

MULTIPLICATION AND DIVISION

Reproducible Skill Builders And Higher Order Thinking Activities Based On NCTM Standards

By Brenda Opie, Lory Jackson, and Douglas McAvinn

Incentive Publications, Inc.
Nashville, Tennessee

Illustrated by Douglas McAvinn
Cover illustration by Douglas McAvinn

ISBN 0-86530-304-5

2 3 4 5 6 7 8 9 10 07 06

PRINTED IN THE UNITED STATES OF AMERICA
www.incentivepublications.com

TABLE OF CONTENTS

FIND AVERAGES

DIVIDING TWO OR THREE DIGIT DIVISORS INTO FOUR OR FIVE DIGIT DIVIDENDS

WHOLE NUMBER PRACTICE; ADDITION, SUBTRACTION, MULTIPLICATION, AND DIVISION

SOLVING WORD PROBLEMS USING ADDITION, SUBTRACTION, MULTIPLICATION, AND DIVISION

DIVISION SPEED TEST

HIGHER LEVEL THINKING ACTIVITIES USING WHOLE NUMBERS

Multiplying one digit factors by two digit factors

NAME________________________

When Big Chief Shortcake died, what did his widow, Golden Straw, say?

DIRECTIONS: First, solve each problem below on another sheet of paper. Second, find your answer in the secret code at the bottom of the page. Third, each time your answer appears in the secret code, write the letter of the problem above it.

Y = 6 x 72 =	U = 7 x 45 =	R = 5 x 12 =
W = 9 x 34 =	B = 2 x 67 =	T = 3 x 42 =
A = 5 x 60 =	O = 8 x 49 =	K = 6 x 48 =
C = 3 x 79 =	S = 6 x 87 =	E = 4 x 73 =
H = 9 x 62 =		

522--126--60--300--306 134--315--60--432

522--558--392--60--126--237--300--288--292

NAME____________________

What did the pony say when he sneezed?

DIRECTIONS: First, solve each problem below on another sheet of paper. Second, find your answer in the secret code at the bottom of the page. Third, each time your answer appears in the secret code, write the letter of the problem above it.

R = 6 x 12 = A = 2 x 38 = M = 7 x 68 =

O = 3 x 15 = L = 9 x 18 = C = 3 x 48 =

X = 7 x 23 = U = 8 x 37 = E = 5 x 37 =

T = 3 x 92 = I = 4 x 15 = S = 9 x 54 =

H = 4 x 65 =

185--161--144--296--486--185 476--185 60

76--476 76 162--60--276--276--162--185

260--45--76--72--486--185

NAME________________________

Why did the lady hold her ears when she walked past the chickens?

DIRECTIONS: First, solve each problem below on another sheet of paper. Second, find your answer in the secret code at the bottom of the page. Third, each time your answer appears in the secret code, write the letter of the problem above it.

F = 6 x 6 x 6 =

G = 5 x 8 x 5 =

R = 5 x 3 x 6 =

L = 4 x 9 x 2 =

W = 7 x 3 x 4 =

T = 1 x 10 x 4 =

N = 9 x 7 x 0 =

O = 7 x 7 x 6 =

I = 9 x 8 x 6 =

D = 7 x 5 x 8 =

H = 8 x 3 x 7 =

S = 8 x 6 x 7 =

U = 4 x 8 x 7 =

A = 9 x 5 x 6 =

C = 3 x 9 x 5 =

E = 5 x 8 x 8 =

B = 9 x 9 x 9 =

729--320--135--270--224--336--320 336--168--320

280--432--280 0--294--40 84--270--0--40 40--294

72--432--336--40--320--0 40--294

40--168--320--432--90 216--294--84--72

72--270--0--200--224--270--200--320

NAME ____________________

What has 18 legs and catches flies?

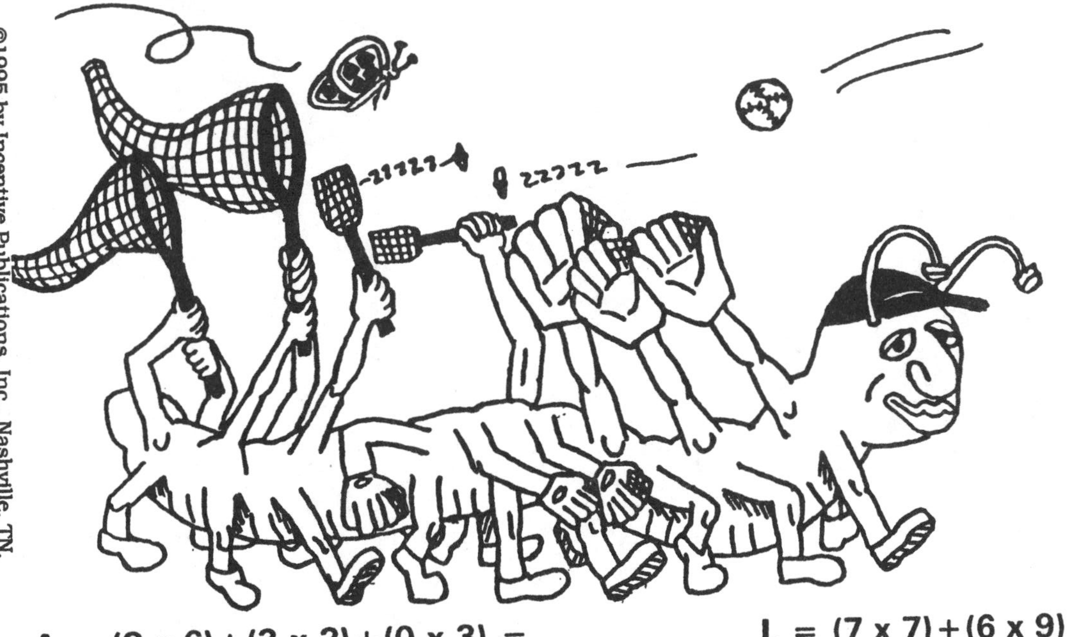

To find the solution to this question, follow these directions. First, work the problems below and find the answer in the answer column. The number in front of the answer tells you where to put the letter of the problem in the row of boxes at the bottom of the page. Work problems on another sheet of paper.

A = (8 x 6) + (3 x 2) + (0 x 3) =

S = (3 x 5) + (7 x 9) + (7 x 8) =

E = (9 x 3) + (4 x 8) + (5 x 9) =

B = (7 x 4) + (10 x 9) + (3 x 1) =

M = (6 x 9) + (3 x 7) + (11 x 2) =

L = (7 x 6) + (0 x 4) + (3 x 3) =

E = (9 x 7) + (4 x 8) + (3 x 2) =

L = (7 x 7) + (6 x 9) + (11 x 4) =

B = (8 x 10) + (4 x 5) + (9 x 5) =

A = (6 x 7) + (5 x 4) + (8 x 3) =

T = (6 x 6) + (8 x 3) + (6 x 3) =

A = (2 x 3) + (7 x 10) + (6 x 11) =

A = (9 x 7) + (5 x 8) + (2 x 1) =

1. 142
2. 145
3. 86
4. 134
5. 104
6. 121
7. 105
8. 51
9. 147
10. 78
11. 101
12. 54
13. 97

1	2	3	4	5	6	7	8	9	10	11	12	13

Multiplying one digit factors by one and two digit factors NAME________________________

Why did the man in jail want to catch the measles?

DIRECTIONS: First, solve each problem below on another sheet of paper. Second, find your answer in the secret code at the bottom of the page. Third, each time your answer appears in the secret code, write the letter of the problem above it.

T = (3 x 4) + (2 x 6) - (3 x 8) =

N = (9 x 7) + (3 x 2) + (8 x 4) =

U = (7 x 8) + (4 x 5) - (9 x 6) =

W = (3 x 11) + (7 x 3) + (6 x 5) =

B = (7 x 6) - (3 x 10) + (9 x 9) =

R = (9 x 10) - (6 x 8) + (5 x 7) =

A = (8 x 8) + (9 x 6) + (8 x 2) =

O = (7 x 4) - (3 x 2) + (6 x 3) =

H = (9 x 11) + (6 x 4) + (5 x 11) =

D = (7 x 8) - (3 x 4) - (2 x 4) =

E = (12 x 2) + (11 x 6) + (7 x 3) =

K = (7 x 9) - (10 x 3) + (6 x 5) =

178--111 84--134--101--0--111--36 0--40

93--77--111--134--63 40--22--0

NAME________________________

What sickness can't you talk about until it's cured?

DIRECTIONS: First, solve each problem below on another sheet of paper. Second, find your answer in the secret code at the bottom of the page. Third, each time your answer appears in the secret code, write the letter of the problem above it.

G = (7 x 23) + (4 x 16) =

Y = (5 x 56) + (3 x 22) =

R = (8 x 49) + (7 x 64) =

A = (3 x 48) - (6 x 10) =

L = (8 x 89) - (3 x 37) =

N = (5 x 86) + (3 x 33) =

K = (6 x 74) - (5 x 30) =

C = (2 x 48) - (3 x 12) =

I = (4 x 13) x (2 x 3) =

S = (9 x 27) x (4 x 2) =

T = (4 x 2) x (4 x 19) =

H = (3 x 44) + (6 x 97) =

E = (8 x 14) - (7 x 11) =

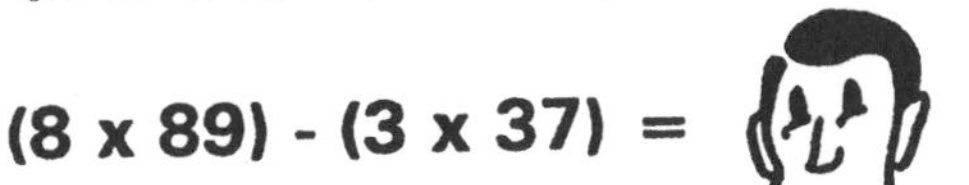

608--714--35

1944--312--60--294--529--35--1944--1944

601--84--840--346--529--225--312--608--312--1944

NAME ____________________

Multiples

DIRECTIONS: Give the first ten multiples of each number:

1. 3: 0, 3, 6, 9, 12, 15, 18, 21, 24, 27
2. 7: ___, ___, ___, ___, ___, ___, ___, ___, ___, ___
3. 5: ___, ___, ___, ___, ___, ___, ___, ___, ___, ___
4. 12: ___, ___, ___, ___, ___, ___, ___, ___, ___, ___
5. 2: ___, ___, ___, ___, ___, ___, ___, ___, ___, ___
6. 4: ___, ___, ___, ___, ___, ___, ___, ___, ___, ___
7. 9: ___, ___, ___, ___, ___, ___, ___, ___, ___, ___
8. 10: ___, ___, ___, ___, ___, ___, ___, ___, ___, ___
9. 8: ___, ___, ___, ___, ___, ___, ___, ___, ___, ___

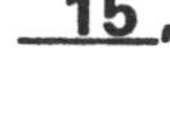

Give the least common multiple for each pair of numbers. The sum total of all the least common multiples should be 357. Add them.

10. 3, 4 12
11. 5, 4 ___
12. 4, 9 ___
13. 3, 7 ___
14. 2, 7 ___
15. 8, 9 ___
16. 5, 10 ___
17. 7, 4 ___
18. 5, 12 ___
19. 2, 8 ___
20. 10, 4 ___
21. 8, 7 ___

NAME______________________________

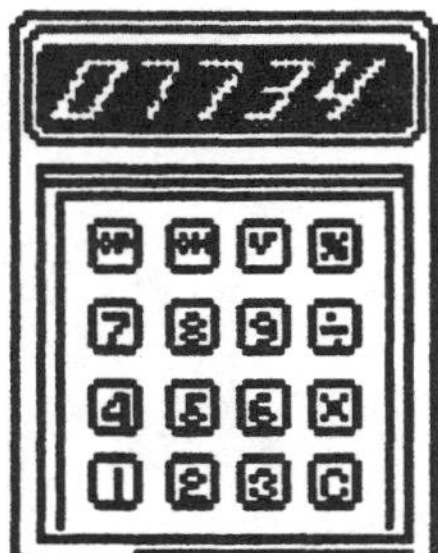

Multiples, Multiples, Multiples

DIRECTIONS: Press these numbers and commands on your calculator:

[0] [+] [1] [1] [=] [=] [=]

It will show 11, 22, 33, ... Each time you press [=], the calculator adds 11 more to the total. This process gives the multiples of 11: 11x1, 11x2, 11x3, and so on. Using your calculator in the manner described, find the first 8 multiples of each of the numbers given below.

1. 8: ______, ______, ______, ______, ______, ______, ______, ______
2. 12: ______, ______, ______, ______, ______, ______, ______, ______
3. 16: ______, ______, ______, ______, ______, ______, ______, ______
4. 13: ______, ______, ______, ______, ______, ______, ______, ______
5. 25: ______, ______, ______, ______, ______, ______, ______, ______
6. 125: ______, ______, ______, ______, ______, ______, ______, ______
7. 14: ______, ______, ______, ______, ______, ______, ______, ______
8. 18: ______, ______, ______, ______, ______, ______, ______, ______
9. 15: ______, ______, ______, ______, ______, ______, ______, ______
10. 38: ______, ______, ______, ______, ______, ______, ______, ______

Multiplying one digit factors by three digit factors

NAME______________________________

What do you get if a dinosaur steps on your foot?

DIRECTIONS: First, solve each problem below on another sheet of paper. Second, find your answer in the secret code at the bottom of the page. Third, each time your answer appears in the secret code, write the letter of the problem above it.

R = 609 x 6 =

S = 908 x 9 =

L = 726 x 4 =

K = 800 x 4 =

N = 742 x 8 =

A = 425 x 6 =

G = 802 x 7 =

E = 900 x 5 =

T = 613 x 7 =

U = 785 x 4 =

O = 375 x 8 =

Y = 599 x 7 =

4193--3000--3140 5614--4500--4291

2550--5936--3200--2904--4500--8172--2550--3140--3654--3140--8172

 NAME________________________________

STATE IDENTIFICATION PUZZLE

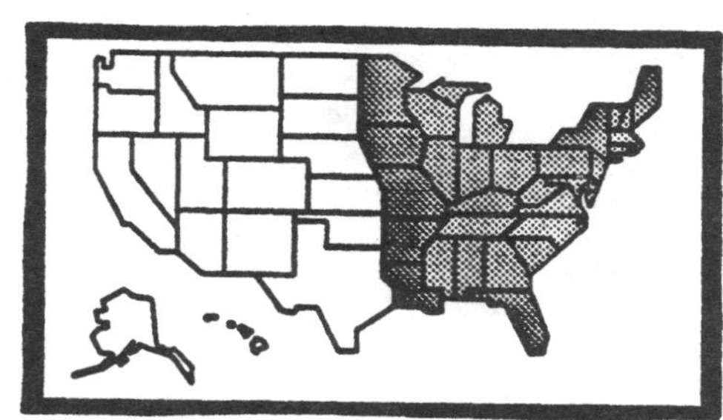

EASTERN UNITED STATES

DIRECTIONS: Work each multiplication problem on another sheet of paper. Then, find your answer on the Eastern States map. Write the name of the state on the map. An example has been done for you.

387 x 5 = <u>1935</u> = Missouri

578 x 9 = ______ = Iowa

707 x 6 = ______ = Indiana

708 x 8 = ______ = Illinois

124 x 3 = ______ = Louisiana

748 x 5 = ______ = Wisconsin

456 x 3 = ______ = West Virginia

603 x 3 = ______ = Kentucky

742 x 5 = ______ = Michigan

800 x 8 = ______ = North Carolina

990 x 6 = ______ = Tennessee

408 x 7 = ______ = Minnesota

599 x 7 = ______ = Alabama

680 x 6 = ______ = Maine

538 x 5 = ______ = Virginia

742 x 8 = ______ = Pennsylvania

493 x 3 = ______ = New York

902 x 4 = ______ = Delaware

807 x 4 = ______ = Mississippi

962 x 5 = ______ = Massachusetts

785 x 4 = ______ = New Hampshire

755 x 8 = ______ = Arkansas

358 x 8 = ______ = Florida

783 x 6 = ______ = Connecticut

467 x 9 = ______ = Georgia

264 x 3 = ______ = South Carolina

819 x 7 = ______ = New Jersey

306 x 3 = ______ = Rhode Island

802 x 7 = ______ = Vermont

736 x 8 = ______ = Ohio

914 x 2 = ______ = Maryland

NAME______________________________

STATE IDENTIFICATION PUZZLE

EASTERN UNITED STATES

NAME________________________

How can you tell a happy motorcyclist?

DIRECTIONS: First, solve each problem below on another sheet of paper. Second, find your answer in the secret code at the bottom of the page. Third, each time your answer appears in the secret code, write the letter of the problem above it.

B = 6 x 734 =

N = 7 x 938 =

H = 5 x 604 =

S = 9 x 326 =

G = 8 x 4321 =

U = 3 x 998 =

Y = 8 x 9702 =

E = 348 x 6 =

I = 807 x 2 =

T = 6 x 9453 =

4404--77,616   56,718--3020--2088

4404--2994--34,568--2934   1614--6566

3020--1614--2934

56,718--2088--2088--56,718--3020

Multiplying one digit factors by three or more digit factors

NAME ____________________

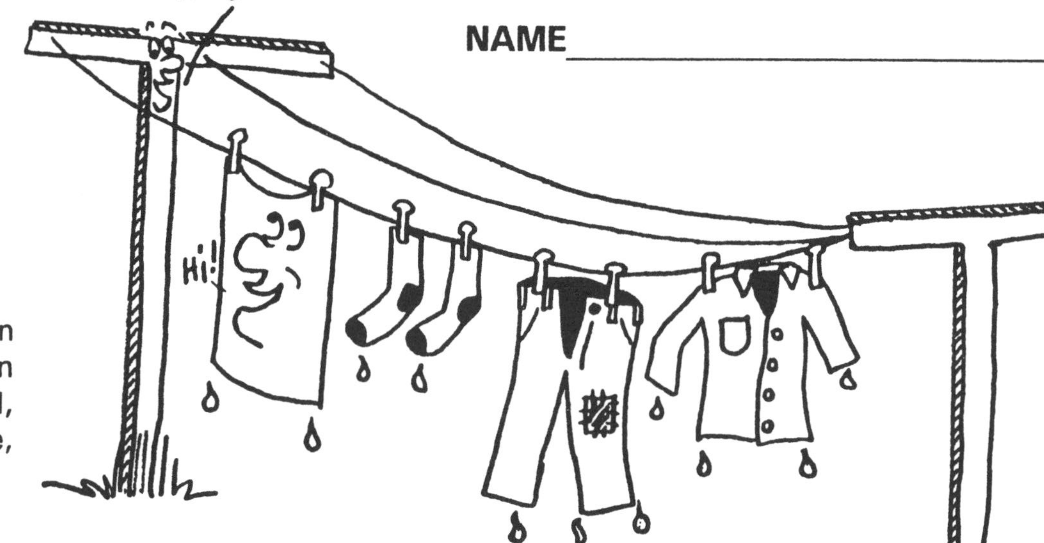

What did the clothesline say to the wet laundry?

DIRECTIONS: First, solve each problem below on another sheet of paper. Second, find your answer in the secret code at the bottom of the page. Third, each time your answer appears in the secret code, write the letter of the problem above it.

H = 7136 x 3 =

D = 74159 x 5 =

T = 50073 x 7 =

R = 39428 x 2 =

I = 60342 x 5 =

Y = 28976 x 7 =

E = 89624 x 3 =

G = 381764 x 6 =

L = 928314 x 9 =

N = 491432 x 8 =

W = 78942 x 8 =

A = 63820 x 4 =

U = 58914 x 6 =

O = 287633 x 9 =

631,536--21,408--202,832   370,795--2,588,697--3,931,456--'--350,511

202,832--2,588,697--353,484   21,408--255,280--3,931,456--2,290,584

255,280--78,856--2,588,697--353,484--3,931,456--370,795

255,280--631,536--21,408--301,710--8,354,826--268,872

NAME________________________________

King Tut's Factor Pyramids - Level 1

DIRECTIONS: Look at the pyramid factor example in the upper left corner. At the top of each pyramid is a number. Fill in the factors of that number in the spaces provided in that pyramid.

15 Finding factors of composite numbers

NAME________________________________

King Tut's Factor Pyramids - Level 2

DIRECTIONS: Look at the pyramid factor example in the upper left corner. At the top of each pyramid is a number. Fill in the factors of that number in the spaces provided in that pyramid.

NAME ______________________

What is the title of this picture?

DIRECTIONS: To find the answer to the riddle, solve each of the problems and locate your answer in the decoder. An example has been done for you.

$5^4 = (5 \times 5) \times (5 \times 5)$

$25 \times 25 = 625$

R = 10^2 = ____________

E = 10^3 = ____________

N = 2^5 = ____________

P = 9^3 = ____________

G = 3^3 = ____________

O = 2^8 = ____________

A = 6^4 = ____________

H = 4^2 = ____________

D = 5^2 = ____________

T = 5^5 = ____________

I = 7^4 = ____________

S = 10^4 = ____________

1296 10,000--729--2401--25--1000--100

25--256--2401--32--27 1296

16--1296--32--25--10,000--3125--1296--32--25

Using exponents

NAME________________________

What did Noah use to see in the dark?

DIRECTIONS: To find the answer to the riddle, solve each of the problems and locate your answer in the decoder. An example has been done for you.

$3^2 \times 5^3 =$ 3 x 3 x 5 x 5 x 5

(3x3) x (5x5) x 5 =

(9x25) x 5 =

225 x 5 = 1125

T = $2^3 \times 4^2 =$

H = $2^8 =$

D = $3^3 \times 5^2 =$

F = $(3^4 - 3^3) \times 10^2 =$

S = $6^3 \times 2^2 \times 3^2 =$

L = $(10^3 \times 3^1) - (9^3 \times 2^2) =$

G = $(7^2 \times 3^3) - (10^3 + 4^3) =$

O = $(4^4 + 5^2) + 70 =$

I = $(7^3 - 6^3) + (10^2 \times 3^1) =$

5,400--84--351--351--675--84--427--259--256--128--7,776

Multiplying factors by multiples of ten or multiples of a hundred **NAME**________________________________

Why is tennis such a noisy game?

DIRECTIONS: First, solve each problem below on another sheet of paper. Second, find your answer in the secret code at the bottom of the page. Third, each time your answer appears in the secret code, write the letter of the problem above it.

T = 627 x 500 =

K = 742 x 600 =

I = 234 x 30 =

R = 295 x 200 =

Y = 412 x 600 =

L = 920 x 600 =

P = 915 x 700 =

A = 642 x 300 =

U = 468 x 400 =

H = 256 x 200 =

S = 519 x 300 =

C = 693 x 40 =

E = 571 x 50 =

B = 573 x 500 =

286,500--28,550--27,720--192,600--187,200--155,700--28,550

28,550--192,600--27,720--51,200

640,500--552,000--192,600--247,200--28,550--59,000

59,000--192,600--7,020--155,700--28,550--155,700 192,600

59,000--192,600--27,720--445,200--28,550--313,500

Multiplying two digit factors by two digit factors

NAME______________________________

What did one math book say to another?

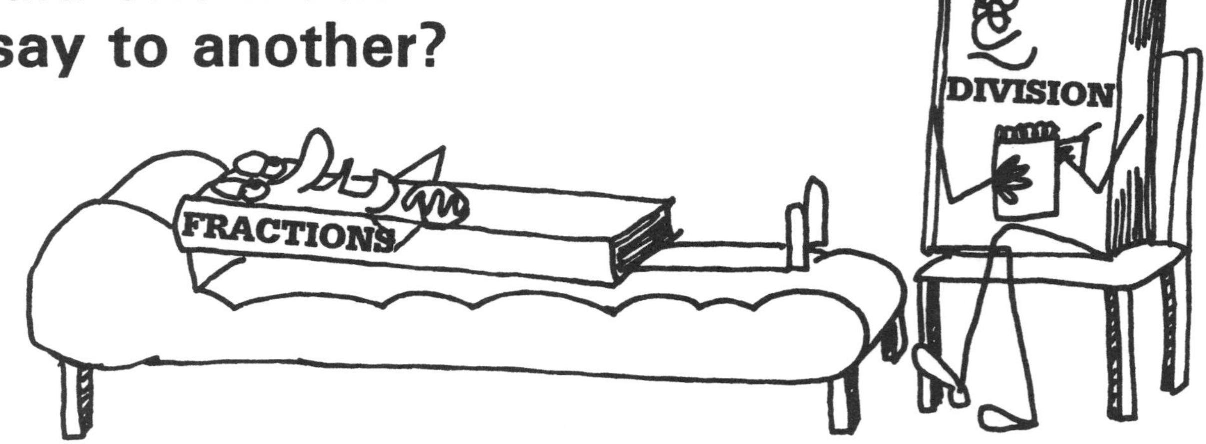

DIRECTIONS: First, solve each problem below on another sheet of paper. Second, find your answer in the secret code at the bottom of the page. Third, each time your answer appears in the secret code, write the letter of the problem above it.

P = 75 x 32 =

R = 78 x 74 =

O = 81 x 74 =

I = 74 x 62 =

A = 96 x 26 =

V = 59 x 19 =

S = 62 x 40 =

D = 37 x 25 =

M = 49 x 49 =

H = 65 x 53 =

B = 37 x 78 =

E = 59 x 47 =

Y = 57 x 36 =

L = 95 x 43 =

2886--5994--2052 925--5994

4588 3445--2496--1121--2773

2400--5772--5994--2886--4085--2773--2401--2480

NAME____________________

What's 8 feet tall, patriotic and flies kites in a rainstorm?

DIRECTIONS: First, solve each problem below on another sheet of paper. Second, find your answer in the secret code at the bottom of the page. Third, each time your answer appears in the secret code, write the letter of the problem above it.

S = 86 x 19 =

J = 67 x 56 =

F = 49 x 49 =

M = 81 x 74 =

E = 67 x 95 =

R = 95 x 43 =

K = 99 x 18 =

N = 63 x 27 =

I = 83 x 45 =

A = 47 x 76 =

B = 62 x 40 =

T = 56 x 78 =

2480--6365--1701--3752--3572--5994--3735--1701

2401--4085--3572--1701--1782--6365--1701--1634--4368--6365--3735--1701

Multiplying three digit factors by two digit factors

NAME________________________

STATE IDENTIFICATION PUZZLE

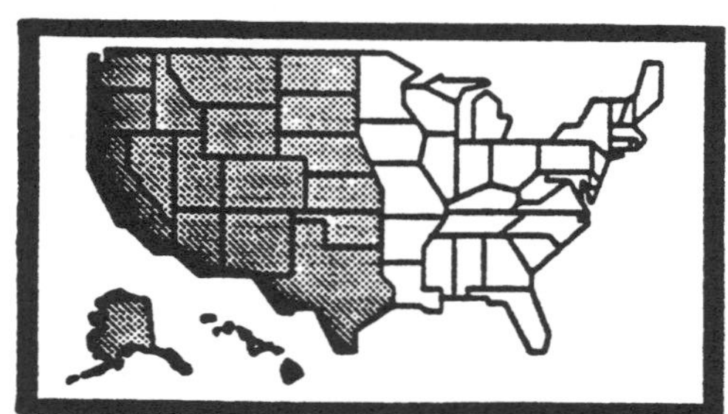

WESTERN UNITED STATES

DIRECTIONS: Work each multiplication problem on another sheet of paper. Then, find your answer on the Western States map. Write the name of the state on the map. An example has been done for you.

372 x 26 = 9672 = Oklahoma

394 x 27 = _______ = Nebraska

756 x 48 = _______ = Arizona

321 x 39 = _______ = Wyoming

298 x 42 = _______ = Hawaii

672 x 70 = _______ = Texas

225 x 88 = _______ = Kansas

803 x 59 = _______ = New Mexico

597 x 76 = _______ = California

809 x 73 = _______ = North Dakota

819 x 39 = _______ = Colorado

659 x 78 = _______ = Nevada

654 x 67 = _______ = Oregon

711 x 32 = _______ = Utah

531 x 21 = _______ = Alaska

759 x 67 = _______ = Washington

159 x 73 = _______ = Montana

630 x 19 = _______ = South Dakota

307 x 15 = _______ = Idaho

NAME____________________________

STATE IDENTIFICATION PUZZLE

WESTERN UNITED STATES

NAME____________________

Why did the President of the United States arrange a meeting with a carpenter?

DIRECTIONS: Estimate each of the products and then find your answer in the secret code. Each time your answer appears in the secret code, write the letter of the problem above it.

1. 43 x 18 = P	6. 253 x 734 = D	11. 55 x 43 = S
2. 435 x 8 = I	7. 348 x 37 = O	12. 11 x 12 = A
3. 67 x 95 = C	8. 69 x 73 = N	13. 9 x 33 = T
4. 563 x 7 = L	9. 378 x 89 = R	14. 398 x 625 = H
5. 834 x 69 = W	10. 34 x 6 = E	15. 13 x 764 = B

240,000--180 56,000--100--4,900--270--180--210,000 270--12,000

36,000--180--800--4,200--100--7,000--180 240,000--3,200--2,400

7,000--100--8,000--3,200--4,900--180--270

NAME________________________

What happened when the male monster met the female monster?

DIRECTIONS: Find the missing factor by using your calculator to estimate. An example has been done for you.

EXAMPLE:

	Product range
☐ x 64	460 to 540

7 x 64 = 448 (too small)
9 x 64 = 576 (too big)
8 x 64 = 512 (just right)

So 8 x 64 is between 460 to 540.

		Product range
1.	☐ x 55 = ☐ (T)	340 to 420
2.	☐ x 83 = ☐ (I)	320 to 480
3.	☐ x 67 = ☐ (A)	150 to 250
4.	☐ x 53 = ☐ (R)	180 to 250
5.	☐ x 12 = ☐ (S)	100 to 115
6.	☐ x 89 = ☐ (O)	100 to 270

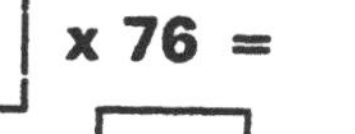

		Product range
7.	☐ x 76 = ☐ (V)	390 to 520
8.	☐ x 33 = ☐ (F)	240 to 280
9.	☐ x 56 = ☐ (G)	50 to 110
10.	☐ x 10 = ☐ (H)	95 to 105
11.	☐ x 9 = ☐ (E)	95 to 105
12.	☐ x 10 = ☐ (L)	125 to 135

13--2--6--11 3--7 8--5--4--9--7 8--4--5--1--10--7

NAME______________________________

What's the difference between a piano and a fish?

DIRECTIONS: First, solve each problem below on another sheet of paper. Second, find your answer in the secret code at the bottom of the page. Third, each time your answer appears in the secret code, write the letter of the problem above it.

H = 374 x 152 =
S = 752 x 364 =
F = 466 x 500 =
T = 589 x 206 =
B = 472 x 575 =

I = 435 x 236 =
P = 572 x 121 =
A = 519 x 309 =
E = 752 x 319 =
N = 950 x 538 =

C = 866 x 304 =
U = 429 x 463 =
O = 705 x 283 =
Y = 384 x 235 =

90,240--199,515--198,627 263,264--160,371--511,100 121,334--198,627--511,100--239,888

160,371 69,212--102,660--160,371--511,100--199,515 271,400--198,627--121,334

90,240--199,515--198,627 263,264--160,371--511,100--511,100--199,515--121,334

121,334--198,627--511,100--160,371 233,000--102,660--273,728--56,848

NAME________________________

What did the bread dough say to the baker?

DIRECTIONS: First, solve each problem below on another sheet of paper. Second, find your answer in the secret code at the bottom of the page. Third, each time your answer appears in the secret code, write the letter of the problem above it.

D = 641 x 348 =

C = 735 x 169 =

T = 436 x 78 =

B = 989 x 99 =

N = 671 x 438 =

I = 902 x 734 =

S = 800 x 945 =

O = 703 x 908 =

K = 684 x 987 =

E = 643 x 807 =

A = 98 x 731 =

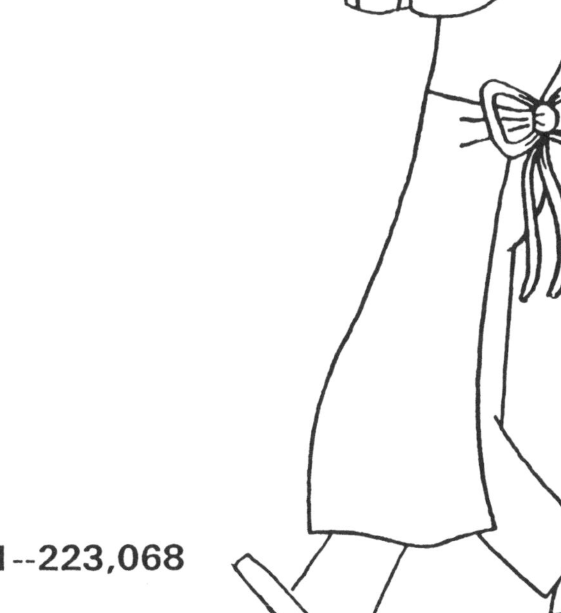

662,068--34,008--'756,000

293,898--662,068--124,215--518,901

34,008--638,324   97,911--518,901

675,108--293,898--518,901--71,638--223,068--518,901--223,068

Multiplying three digit factors by three or more digit factors

NAME ______________________

Why did the chimney call the doctor?

DIRECTIONS: First, solve each problem below on another sheet of paper. Second, find your answer in the secret code at the bottom of the page. Third, each time your answer appears in the secret code, write the letter of the problem above it.

L = 846 x 208 =

D = 6174 x 68 =

F = 883 x 327 =

Y = 468 x 126 =

N = 752 x 368 =

I = 714 x 329 =

M = 298 x 42 =

H = 7265 x 45 =

S = 654 x 395 =

A = 678 x 386 =

U = 832 x 642 =

C = 257 x 103 =

E = 818 x 514 =

B = 8953 x 765 =

T = 3659 x 428 =

6,849,045--420,452--26,471--261,708--534,144--258,330--420,452

1,566,052--326,925--420,452

26,471--326,925--234,906--12,516--276,736--420,452--58,968

326,925--261,708--419,832 1,566,052--326,925--420,452

288,741--175,968--534,144--420,452

Multiplying three digit factors by three or more digit factors **NAME**________________________________

Why did the nuclear powered robot break down?

DIRECTIONS: First, solve each problem below on another sheet of paper. Second, find your answer in the secret code at the bottom of the page. Third, each time your answer appears in the secret code, write the letter of the problem above it.

D = 7894 x 634 =

C = 8043 x 896 =

A = 783 x 6025 =

O = 8632 x 7854 =

I = 843 x 609 =

E = 9952 x 6439 =

H = 3218 x 9572 =

M = 6003 x 2075 =

T = 521 x 345 =

30,802,696--64,080,928

30,802,696--4,717,575--5,004,796

4,717,575--179,745--67,795,728--12,456,225--513,387--7,206,528

4,717,575--7,206,528--30,802,696--64,080,928

NAME______________________________

Lattice Multiplication

BACKGROUND INFORMATION: Lattice multiplication was first written about 1478 in Italy and was called "Gelosia" or lattice. Here is how one could use this method to multiply 375 x 643:

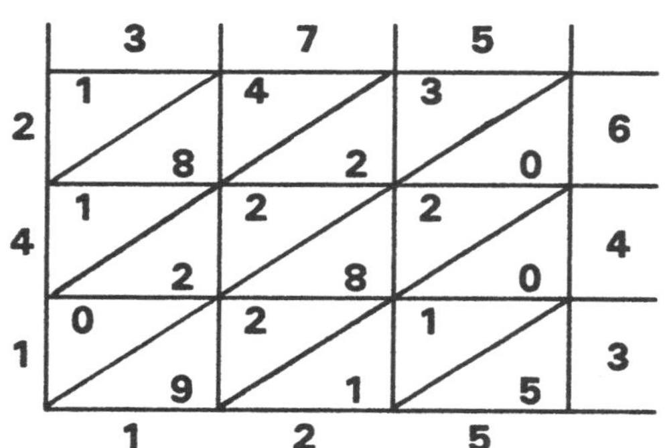

Notice in the upper right square is the product of 5 and 6, 30. To its immediate left is the product of 7 and 6, 42. Other products are calculated in the same way. The final product is found by adding numbers along the diagonals, starting with the lower right square and regrouping to the next diagonal where necessary. The product of 375 and 643 is 241,125.

DIRECTIONS: Complete these lattice multiplication problems using the explanation given above.

1. 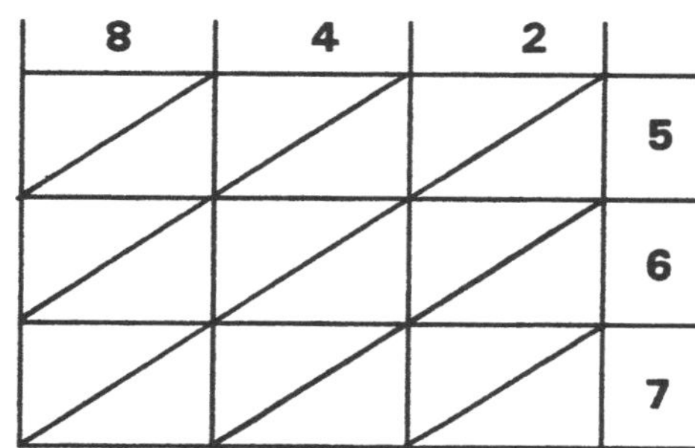

4. 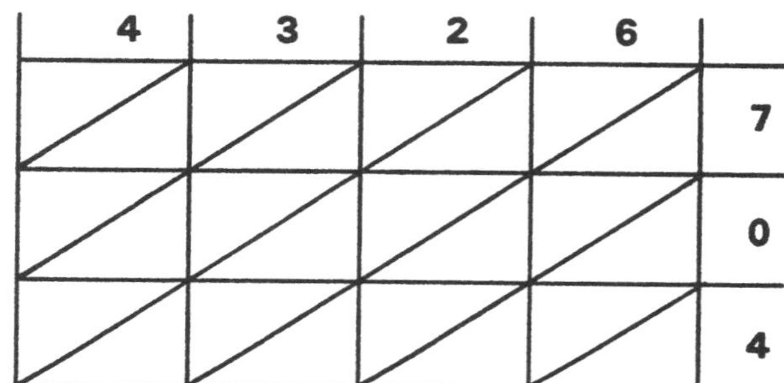

2. 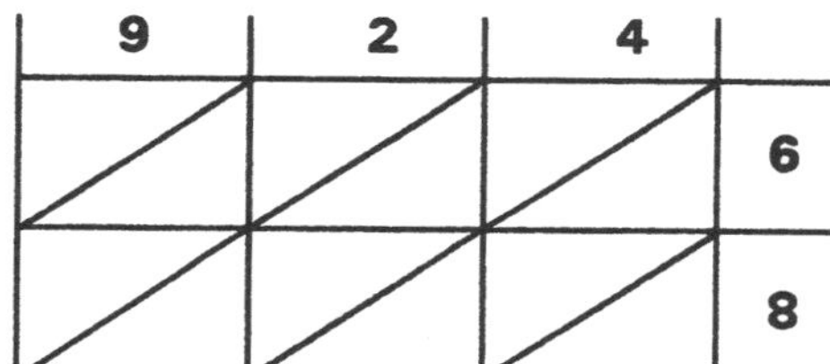

5. 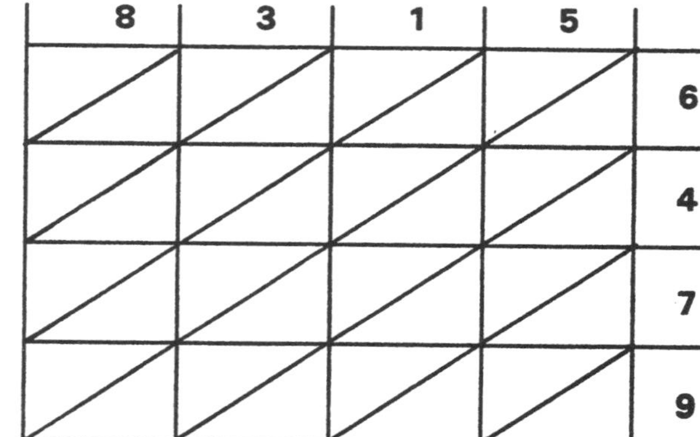

3. 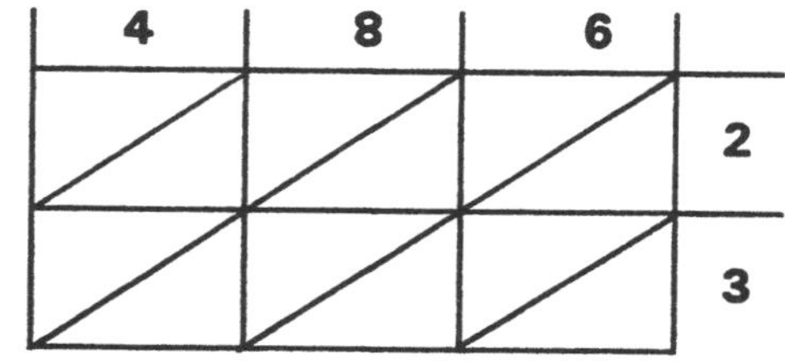

SUPER CHALLENGE: Make your own lattice boards and solve these problems:

(A) 64,395 x 1462 **(B) 743,692 x 38402**

NAME____________________________

Multiplication Calculator Activities

ACTIVITY ONE

DIRECTIONS: Find the largest number when multiplied by itself has a product equal to the number given. An example has been done for you.

EXAMPLE: 7225 = 85 x 85

1. 3136 = ________________
2. 576 = ________________
3. 3969 = ________________
4. 2401 = ________________
5. 5476 = ________________
6. 441 = ________________
7. 1024 = ________________
8. 9216 = ________________
9. 14,884 = ________________ (Bonus)

ACTIVITY TWO

DIRECTIONS: Use your calculator to find the missing digits in the following multiplication problems. An example has been done for you.

EXAMPLE:

```
   3 3 4          3 3 4
 x   2 5        x   2 5
 1 _ 7 0        1 6 7 0      5 x 334 = 1670
 6 _ 8 0      + 6 6 8 0      20 x 334 = 6680
 8 _ 5 0        8 3 5 0      1670 + 6680 = 8350
```

```
1.      7 3 9
      x   4 6
      4 4 _ 4
  + 2 _ 5 6 0
    3 _ 9 _ 4
```

```
2.      4 5 6 3
      x     8 5
      _ 2 _ 1 5
  + 3 _ 5 0 _ 0
    3 _ 7 _ 5 5
```

```
3.          8 9 4 3
          x   6 5 2
          1 _ 8 8 _
        _ 4 _ 1 _ 0
  + _ _ 6 5 8 0 0
      5 _ 3 _ 8 _ 6
```

```
4.        6   9   3
        x 8   4   2
          1   3   8 _
      2 _ 7 _ 0
  + _ 5 4 _ 0 0
    5 _ 3 _ 0   6
```

```
5.        7 9 1 4
        x   7 3 8
        6 _ _ 1 2
      2 _ 7 4 2 0
  + _ 5 3 9 8 _ 0
    5 _ 4 _ 5 _ 2
```

NAME________________________________

What is the minister doing when he rehearses his sermon?

DIRECTIONS: To find the answer to the riddle, solve each of the problems and locate your answer in the decoder. Work your problems on another sheet of paper.

1. How many minutes are in 8 hours? ________ = N
2. How many seconds are in 7 minutes? _______ = G
3. How many hours are in 6 days? ________ = W
4. There are 144 nails in 1 box. How many nails are in 6 boxes? ________ = T
5. A school bus seats 46 passengers. How many passengers will 9 such buses seat? ________ = S
6. How many ounces are in 50 pounds? ________ = C
7. There are 36 exposures on 1 roll of film. How many pictures can you take with 5 roles of this film? ________ = A
8. There were 15 players on a soccer team. Each player sold 10 tickets. How many tickets did the team sell? ________ = R
9. If there are 36 cookies in one box, how many cookies will there be in 30 boxes? ______ = P
10. David can read 24 pages in an hour. How many pages can he read in 11 hours? ______ = I
11. If 1 ticket to a play cost $5.35 how much will 6 tickets cost? _____ = E
12. A farmer planted 26 tomato plants in each of 30 rows. How many tomato plants did he plant? ________ = H

780--$32.10 264--414 1080--150--180--800--864--264--800--264--480--420

144--780--180--846 780--$32.10

1080--150--$32.10--180--800--780--$32.10--414

NAME____________________

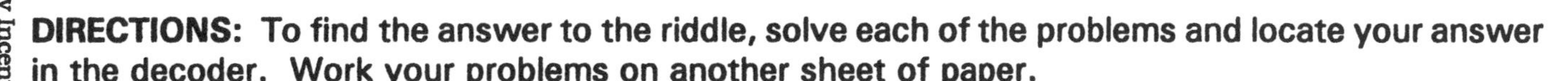

Where do moles get married?

DIRECTIONS: To find the answer to the riddle, solve each of the problems and locate your answer in the decoder. Work your problems on another sheet of paper.

1. Find the cost of 4 dozen books at $1.40 for each book. ________ = U
2. If sweet corn is selling 2 ears for 50 cents, find the cost of 2 dozen ears. ________ = L
3. John bought 3 packages of notebook paper. In each package there were 390 sheets. How many total sheets did John have? ________ = A
4. Kristy decided to save 75 cents each day. How much money did she save in one year? ________ = O
5. Abbie bought 3 dozen apples at $1.35 a dozen. How much change should she receive from a ten dollar bill? ______ = T
6. Find the cost of 150 gallons of fuel oil at 79 cents a gallon. ________ = V
7. At a neighborhood refreshment stand, Kevin made $3.25. Chris tripled that amount. How much did Chris make? ______ = F
8. How much change should Jenny receive from a $15 bill if she bought 12 twenty-five cent stamps, 4 fifteen cent stamps and 15 one cent stamps? ________ = I
9. In a movie theater there were 65 rows of seats with 23 seats in each row. How many seats are in the theater? ______ = E
10. Erin bought 2 gallons of ice cream for $1.79 each and 1 bag of cookies for $1.39. How much change should she receive from a 10 dollar bill? ________ = N

\$11.25--\$5.03 1170 \$5.95--\$67.20--\$5.03--\$5.03--1495--\$6.00

\$273.75--\$9.75 \$6.00--\$273.75--\$118.50--1495

NAME______________________

Why did the detective arrest the baseball player?

DIRECTIONS: To find the answer to the riddle, solve each of the problems and locate your answer in the decoder. Work your problems on another sheet of paper.

1. The great brown bear of Alaska weighs about 1,500 lbs. How many pounds would 7 brown bears weigh? ________ = F
2. A bat has wings of skin instead of feathers and devours insects for its diet. How many bugs will it eat if it eats 130 bugs every day for nine days? ________ = D
3. An amazing fact is that crickets can tell us the Fahrenheit temperature by counting the number of cricket chirps in 14 seconds and then adding 40 to the number of chirps. If a cricket chirps 20 times in 14 seconds, what is the temperature? ________ = T
4. The elephant uses its powerful trunk to pull down trees. If it pulls down 7 trees a day, how many trees will it pull down in 3 weeks? ________ = S
5. The longest living invertebrate in the insect world is the termite queen. She has been known to live 50 years. During that time she can lay over 30,000 eggs every day. How many eggs can she lay in 1 year? ________ = L
6. Baleen whales, large mammals, can stay under water for as long as 40 minutes without coming to the surface for air. How many minutes do 12 whales stay under water at 40 minutes each? ________ = E
7. A hummingbird has the fewest number of feathers in the bird kingdom with only 950, while the whistling swan has the most with 25,216. The hummingbird can beat its wings 90 times a second. How many times will it beat its wings in 8 seconds? ________ = R
8. A wolf can run continuously for several hours at a speed of 20 miles per hour. How far can a wolf run in 8 hours? ________ = H
9. Lions prefer larger animals for their food: zebras, antelopes and buffalo. If a male lion can eat 75 pounds of meat in one meal, how many pounds can he eat in 6 meals? ________ = B
10. A newborn baby kangaroo is called a joey and measures about 1 inch at birth. A joey remains in its mother's pouch for about 8 months. If each month has 30 days, how long will the joey stay in its mother's pouch before coming out and being on its own? ________ = O
11. The salmon travels 2,000 miles to lay her eggs. How many total miles would a school of 60 salmon travel at 2,000 miles each? ________ = A

160--480 160--480--120,000--720--1170 60--160--120,000--60 160--480 147--60--240--10,950,000--480

120,000 10,950,000--240--60 240--10,500 450--120,000--147--480--147

NAME________________________

Why shouldn't you mention the number 288 aloud in front of the principal?

DIRECTIONS: To find the answer to the riddle, solve each of the problems and locate your answer in the decoder. Work your problems on another sheet of paper. Some of these problems may require more than one operation.

1. There are 43 classes in the Simpson School. Each class has 28 students. If 35 students are absent, how many students are present? _______ = G
2. A classroom ordered 23 books that cost $8.95 each and 8 balls that cost $6.30 each. What was the total amount of the order? _______ = O
3. How many days are in 45 years? _______ = W
4. In an auditorium there are 24 rows with 32 seats in each row and 22 rows with 35 seats in each row. How many seats are there in all? _____ = I
5. Captain Alpern flies an airliner between San Francisco and Atlanta, a distance of 2,345 miles. In 6 round trips, how far would he fly? _______ = R
6. How many ounces are in 16-1/2 pounds? _______ = M
7. If Erin bought 3 books at $7.95 each, a record player for $59.86, and 2 records for $8.98 each, how much did she spend all together? _____ = N
8. In 1962 Wilt Chamberlain averaged about 50 points in a game. At that rate, how many points did he score in 15 games? _______ = H
9. How many hours are in 150 days? _______ = T
10. Abbie bought 2 bags of birdseed for $2.95 each, and 1 bag of cat food for $5.95. How much change should she receive from $20.00? _______ = S
11. If tickets for a basketball game cost $2.50 each, how much would 12 tickets cost? _______ = C
12. How many minutes are in 64 hours? _______ = E
13. Scott bought 2 packages of notebook paper for $1.79 each. He gave the clerk $10.00. How much change did he get back? _______ = B
14. Robert has $8.40. He returned 48 soda bottles for 4¢ each. He bought a baseball for $7.95. How much money did he have left? ________ = A
15. How many pints are in 34-1/2 gallons? _______ = U

$6.42--3840--$30.00--$2.37--276--$8.15--3840 3600--750--3840

$101.67--276--264--$6.42--3840--28,140 1538--$8.15

3600--16,425--$256.25 1169--28,140--$256.25--$8.15--$8.15

MULTIPLICATION FACTS SPEED TEST (0-12)

NAME____________________

DATE____________________

SCORE____________________
(100 Facts)

0 x 5 =
3 x 9 =
4 x 6 =
1 x 12 =
5 x 8 =
6 x 9 =
1 x 1 =
7 x 8 =
8 x 9 =
4 x 7 =
0 x 11 =
3 x 10 =
2 x 8 =
5 x 1 =
1 x 11 =
5 x 11 =
2 x 7 =
7 x 11 =
1 x 10 =
8 x 6 =
4 x 2 =
5 x 12 =
8 x 7 =
6 x 1 =
4 x 3 =
4 x 5 =
6 x 11 =
2 x 10 =
5 x 9 =

6 x 10 =
1 x 2 =
4 x 11 =
6 x 8 =
3 x 11 =
3 x 5 =
7 x 9 =
0 x 10 =
7 x 10 =
3 x 4 =
8 x 12 =
5 x 2 =
10 x 11 =
4 x 10 =
5 x 10 =
7 x 2 =
5 x 3 =
1 x 9 =
7 x 3 =
3 x 12 =
8 x 8 =
6 x 2 =
2 x 9 =
0 x 12 =
4 x 4 =
5 x 7 =
8 x 3 =
10 x 10 =
6 x 12 =

4 x 12 =
9 x 4 =
3 x 6 =
1 x 8 =
11 x 11 =
6 x 7 =
7 x 4 =
8 x 1 =
2 x 2 =
5 x 4 =
3 x 3 =
2 x 10 =
6 x 3 =
8 x 12 =
0 x 8 =
6 x 4 =
9 x 8 =
9 x 11 =
9 x 12 =
5 x 6 =
7 x 7 =
2 x 12 =
8 x 5 =
7 x 6 =
12 x 11 =
7 x 5 =
3 x 7 =
1 x 5 =
8 x 4 =

8 x 11 =
2 x 11 =
4 x 8 =
9 x 6 =
6 x 6 =
5 x 5 =
9 x 5 =
3 x 8 =
7 x 12 =
6 x 5 =
4 x 9 =
3 x 2 =
8 x 10 =

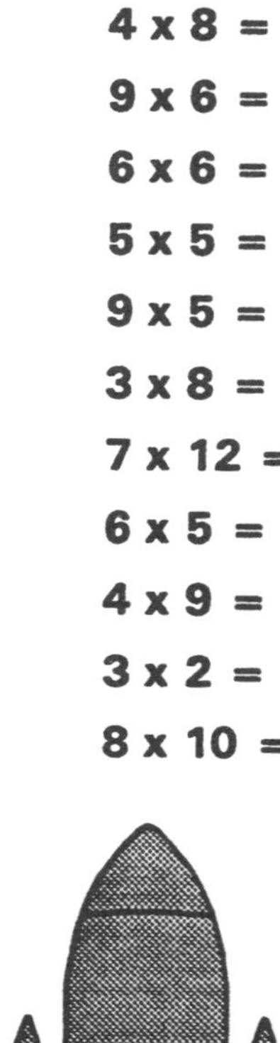

NAME____________________

Where do polar bears vote?

To find the solution to this question, follow these directions. First, work the problems below and find the answer in the answer column. The number in front of the answer tells you where to put the letter of the problem in the row of boxes at the bottom of the page. Work problems on another sheet of paper.

N = 90 ÷ 6 =

H = 72 ÷ 6 =

P = 88 ÷ 8 =

R = 87 ÷ 3 =

O = 98 ÷ 7 =

E = 78 ÷ 6 =

T = 48¢ ÷ 3 =

H = 64 ÷ 2 =

A = 76¢ ÷ 4 =

L = 52 ÷ 2 =

O = 90¢ ÷ 5 =

E = 88 ÷ 4 =

T = 84 ÷ 4 =

T = 84 ÷ 3 =

1. 19¢
2. 28
3. 21
4. 32
5. 22
6. 15
7. 14
8. 29
9. 16¢
10. 12
11. 11
12. 18¢
13. 26
14. 13

1	2	3	4	5	6	7	8	9	10	11	12	13	14

Dividing by one digit divisors

NAME________________________

What did one wall say to the other wall?

DIRECTIONS: First, solve each problem below on another sheet of paper. Second, find your answer in the secret code at the bottom of the page. Third, each time your answer appears in the code, write the letter of the problem above it.

R = (54 ÷ 9) + (81 ÷ 9) + (28 ÷ 7) =

T = (49 ÷ 7) + (25 ÷ 5) + (30 ÷ 5) =

Y = (20 ÷ 4) + (15 ÷ 5) + (16 ÷ 16) =

O = (50 ÷ 2) + (30 ÷ 3) + (18 ÷ 2) =

N = (18 ÷ 3) + (21 ÷ 3) + (8 ÷ 4) =

H = (9 ÷ 9) + (12 ÷ 3) + (72 ÷ 8) =

U = (90 ÷ 10) + (81 ÷ 9) + (20 ÷ 2) =

L = (42 ÷ 7) + (36 ÷ 6) + (30 ÷ 2) =

M = (10 ÷ 5) + (50 ÷ 2) + (12 ÷ 4) =

W = (54 ÷ 6) + (24 ÷ 8) + (100 ÷ 4) =

E = (15 ÷ 5) + (90 ÷ 6) + (16 ÷ 8) =

I = (40 ÷ 8) + (16 ÷ 4) + (30 ÷ 2) =

C = (24 ÷ 6) + (8 ÷ 8) + (9 ÷ 3) =

A = (32 ÷ 4) + (34 ÷ 2) + (72 ÷ 9) =

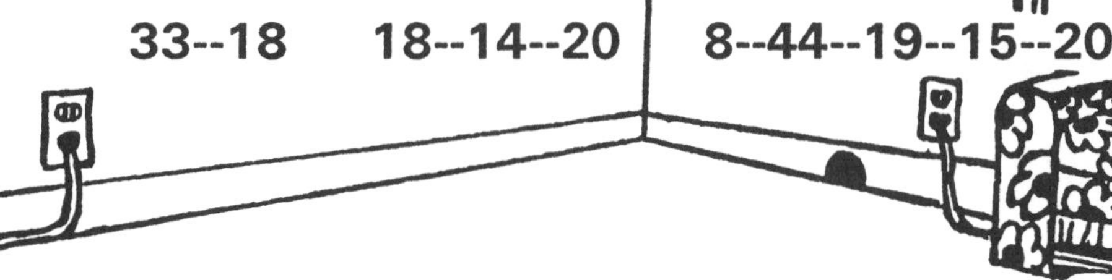

24 37--24--27--27 30--20--20--18 9--44--28

33--18 18--14--20 8--44--19--15--20--19

NAME______________________

What time do ducks get up in the morning?

DIRECTIONS: First, solve each problem below on another sheet of paper. Second, find you answer in the secret code at the bottom of the page. Third, each time your answer appears in the code, write the letter of the problem above it.

Q = 315 ÷ 7 =	N = 168 ÷ 3 =	D = 315 ÷ 5 =
C = 747 ÷ 3 =	A = 784 ÷ 2 =	E = 396 ÷ 4 =
T = 832 ÷ 8 =	H = 412 ÷ 4 =	U = 848 ÷ 4 =
K = 360 ÷ 6 =	F = 679 ÷ 7 =	O = 408 ÷ 4 =
W = 840 ÷ 2 =		

392--104 104--103--99 45--212--392--249--60 102--97 63--392--420--56

NAME________________________________

What is the difference between a dog and a marine biologist?

DIRECTIONS: First, solve each problem below on another sheet of paper. Second, find your answer in the secret code at the bottom of the page. Third, each time your answer appears in the code, write the letter of the problem above it.

R = 297 ÷ 3 =

G = 270 ÷ 6 =

N = 196 ÷ 2 =

T = 120 ÷ 8 =

S = 450 ÷ 6 =

L = 238 ÷ 7 =

H = 152 ÷ 8 =

I = 152 ÷ 4 =

W = 294 ÷ 6 =

D = 539 ÷ 7 =

A = 475 ÷ 5 =

O = 332 ÷ 4 =

E = 142 ÷ 2 =

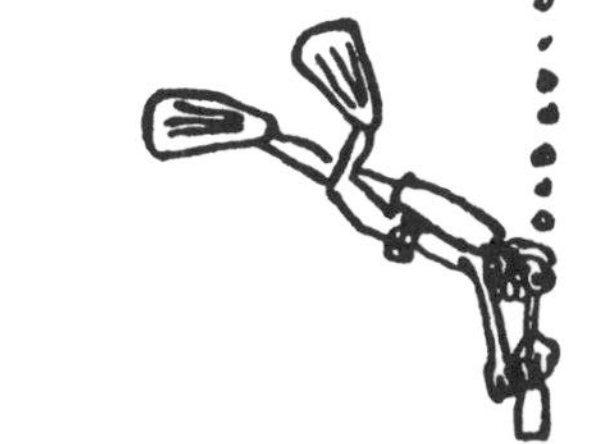

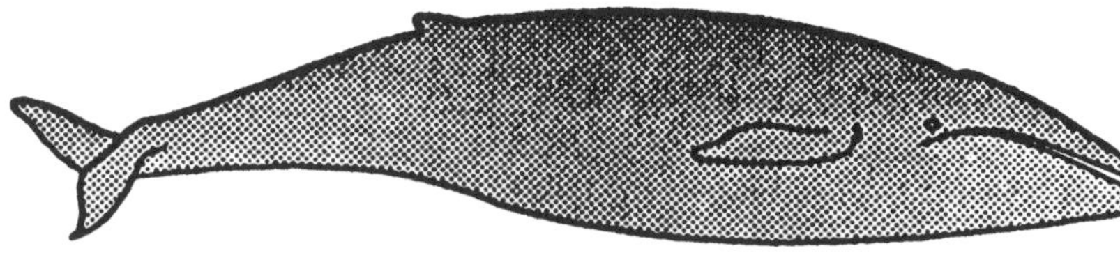

83--98--71 49--95--45--75 95 15--95--38--34 95--98--77 15--19--71

83--15--19--71--99 15--95--45--75 95 49--19--95--34--71

NAME______________________

What kind of car do rich rock stars drive?

To find the solution to this question, follow these directions. First, work the problems below and find the answer in the answer column. The number in front of the answer tells you where to put the letter of the problem in the row of boxes at the bottom of the page. Work problems on another sheet of paper.

K = 4146 ÷ 6 =	R = 3818 ÷ 6 =	1. 703 R2	7. 1192 R1	13. 239 R2
R = 2815 ÷ 4 =	E = 2755 ÷ 5 =	2. 703 R3	8. 858 R3	14. 300 R3
D = 5151 ÷ 6 =	O = 3072 ÷ 4 =	3. 760 R2	9. 636 R2	15. 768
S = 1675 ÷ 7 =	C = 9314 ÷ 9 =	4. 382	10. 903	16. 941
Y = 7528 ÷ 8 =	N = 7153 ÷ 6 =	5. 691	11. 906	17. 1034 R8
C = 3438 ÷ 9 =	O = 5418 ÷ 6 =	6. 720 R2	12. 4837	18. 551
L = 5436 ÷ 6 =	L = 9674 ÷ 2 =			
A = 2882 ÷ 4 =	R = 2403 ÷ 8 =			
O = 3042 ÷ 4 =	A = 3517 ÷ 5 =			

1	2	3	4	5	6	7	8	9	10	11	12	13	14	15	16	17	18

Estimating quotients

NAME________________________________

What do you find on a mouse's cheek after he's been spanked?

DIRECTIONS: Estimate each of the quotients. Locate your answer in the decoder and each time your answer appears in the decoder, write the letter of the problem above it.

1. $4\overline{)347}$ = K

2. $7\overline{)792}$ = S

3. $3\overline{)3641}$ = A

4. $4\overline{)14,396}$ = U

5. $4\overline{)2498}$ = T

6. $7\overline{)45,673}$ = E

7. $4\overline{)16,573}$ = R

8. $6\overline{)4882}$ = O

9. $3\overline{)26,792}$ = M

8000--800--3000--100--6000 — 80--1000 — 600--6000--1000--4000--100

NAME________________________

What did the pencil say to the pencil sharpener?

DIRECTIONS: First, solve each problem below on another sheet of paper. Second, find your answer in the secret code at the bottom of the page. Third, each time your answer appears in the secret code, write the letter of the problem above it.

S = 690 ÷ 23 =

N = 578 ÷ 34 =

U = 294 ÷ 98 =

T = 483 ÷ 69 =

H = 190 ÷ 10 =

G = 847 ÷ 77 =

O = 806 ÷ 13 =

D = 306 ÷ 17 =

P = 600 ÷ 24 =

C = 544 ÷ 17 =

L = 370 ÷ 74 =

R = 840 ÷ 35 =

I = 156 ÷ 12 =

E = 285 ÷ 19 =

A = 186 ÷ 93 =

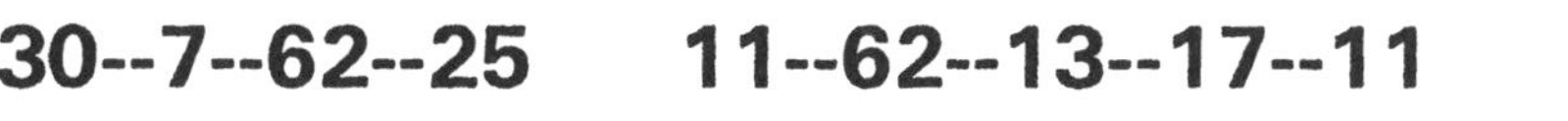

30--7--62--25 11--62--13--17--11

2--24--62--3--17--18 13--17

32--13--24--32--5--15--30 2--17--18

11--15--7 7--62 7--19--15 25--62--13--17--7

Why did the ram fall over the cliff?

DIRECTIONS: First, solve each problem below and find your answer in the secret code at the bottom of the page. Second, each time your answer appears in the secret code, write the letter of the problem above it.

W = 370 ÷ 74 =

R = 990 ÷ 22 =

H = 228 ÷ 19 =

T = 754 ÷ 26 =

D = 180 ÷ 18 =

S = 316 ÷ 79 =

I = 377 ÷ 29 =

N = 784 ÷ 56 =

O = 806 ÷ 13 =

U = 518 ÷ 14 =

E = 297 ÷ 99 =

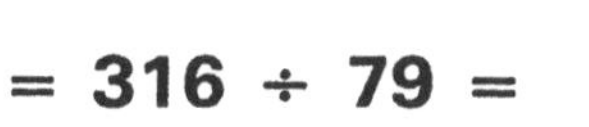

12--3 10--13--10 14--62--29 4--3--3 29--12--3 3--5--3 29--37--45--14

NAME________________________

Why did the house call for a doctor?

DIRECTIONS: First, solve each problem below on another sheet of paper. Second, find your answer in the secret code at the bottom of the page. Third, each time your answer appears in the code, write the letter of the problem above it.

W = 690 ÷ 23 =

P = 540 ÷ 15 =

B = 667 ÷ 23 =

H = 845 ÷ 13 =

I = 704 ÷ 16 =

D = 576 ÷ 96 =

U = 925 ÷ 25 =

A = 736 ÷ 46 =

C = 860 ÷ 86 =

T = 559 ÷ 43 =

S = 420 ÷ 15 =

N = 646 ÷ 17 =

E = 754 ÷ 29 =

O = 817 ÷ 19 =

29--26--10--16--37--28--26 44--13

65--16--6 30--44--38--6--43--30 36--16--38--26--28

NAME________________________

Why did the bowling pins lie down?

DIRECTIONS: First, find the missing factor in each equation below and find your answer in the code. Second, each time the answer appears in the secret code, write the letter in that problem above it.

1. C x 13 = 559

   C =

2. R x 63 = 630

   R =

3. T x 84 = 4788

   T =

4. O x 24 = 7656

   O =

5. N x 50 = 7800

   N =

6. A x 22 = 880

   A =

7. H x 44 = 4268

   H =

8. W x 25 = 625

   W =

9. B x 64 = 2496

   B =

10. U x 30 = 9510

    U =

11. E x 24 = 768

    E =

12. S x 66 = 5082

    S =

13. I x 34 = 714

    I =

14. Y x 88 = 7744

    Y =

15. K x 15 = 1275

    K =

HEY, GET UP!

39--32--43--40--317--77--32 57--97--32--88

25--32--10--32 319--156 77--57--10--21--85--32

NAME________________________

Do rabbits use combs?

To find the solution to this question, follow these directions. First, work the problems below and find the answer in the answer column. The number in front of the answer tells you where to put the letter of the problem in the row of boxes at the bottom of the page. Work problems on another sheet of paper.

Y = 2834 ÷ 25 =

H = 9035 ÷ 42 =

B = 8935 ÷ 43 =

U = 4119 ÷ 96 =

S = 7136 ÷ 32 =

T = 9012 ÷ 31 =

N = 9284 ÷ 64 =

E = 2815 ÷ 47 =

A = 1085 ÷ 35 =

H = 4346 ÷ 48 =

R = 5696 ÷ 85 =

S = 2496 ÷ 64 =

U = 4019 ÷ 59 =

E = 5082 ÷ 66 =

O = 7658 ÷ 24 =

H = 4916 ÷ 36 =

S = 2444 ÷ 72 =

R = 3488 ÷ 87 =

E = 1710 ÷ 18 =

E = 1074 ÷ 43 =

1. 145 R4
2. 319 R2
3. 290 R22
4. 90 R26
5. 59 R42
6. 113 R9
7. 68 R7
8. 39
9. 95
10. 215 R5
11. 31
12. 67 R1
13. 24 R42
14. 207 R34
15. 40 R8
16. 42 R87
17. 33 R68
18. 136 R20
19. 77
20. 223

1	2	3	4	5	6	7	8	9	10	11	12	13	14	15	16	17	18	19	20

NAME________________________

Why did the jogger go see the veterinarian?

DIRECTIONS: First, solve all the problems below to find the missing factors. Second, each time the answer appears in the secret code, write the letter in that problem above it.

1. H x 58 = 986

   H =

2. C x 76 = 608

   C =

3. L x 53 = 4717

   L =

4. R x 22 = 990

   R =

5. U x 41 = 3034

   U =

6. V x 26 = 754

   V =

7. I x 41 = 2624

   I =

8. S x 89 = 3916

   S =

9. T x 24 = 840

   T =

10. A x 12 = 384

    A =

11. E x 99 = 6039

    E =

12. B x 13 = 806

    B =

62--61--8--32--74--44--61 17--64--44 8--32--89--29--61--44 17--74--45--35

NAME________________________

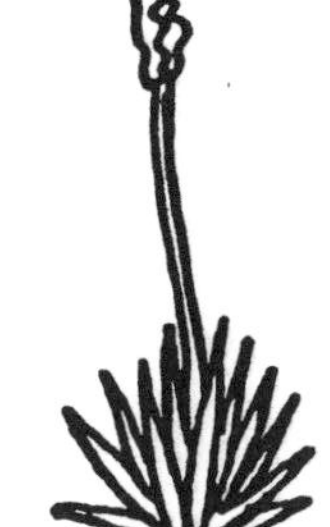

What plants are the greediest?

DIRECTIONS: First, solve each problem below on another sheet of paper. Second, find your answer in the secret code at the bottom of the page. Third, each time your answer appears in the code, write the letter of the problem above it.

G = 3354 ÷ 78 =

N = 8712 ÷ 99 =

Y = 6324 ÷ 68 =

M = 4982 ÷ 94 =

W = 3572 ÷ 76 =

D = 5082 ÷ 66 =

T = 805 ÷ 35 =

H = 4712 ÷ 76 =

I = 2888 ÷ 76 =

R = 9044 ÷ 76 =

A = 4512 ÷ 47 =

K = 6365 ÷ 67 =

V = 1989 ÷ 51 =

C = 6318 ÷ 78 =

L = 1260 ÷ 30 =

S = 3040 ÷ 76 =

E = 4256 ÷ 76 =

47--56--56--77--40, 43--38--39--56

23--62--56--53 96--88 38--88--81--62 96--88--77 23--62--56--93

47--38--42--42 23--96--95--56 96 93--96--119--77

Dividing with a calculator

NAME ______________________

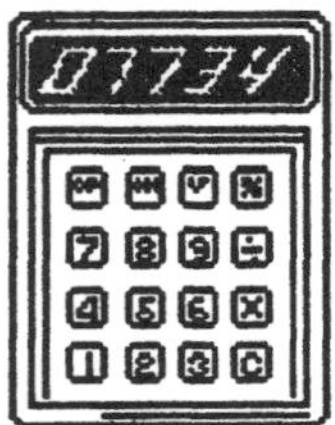

What is the title of this picture?

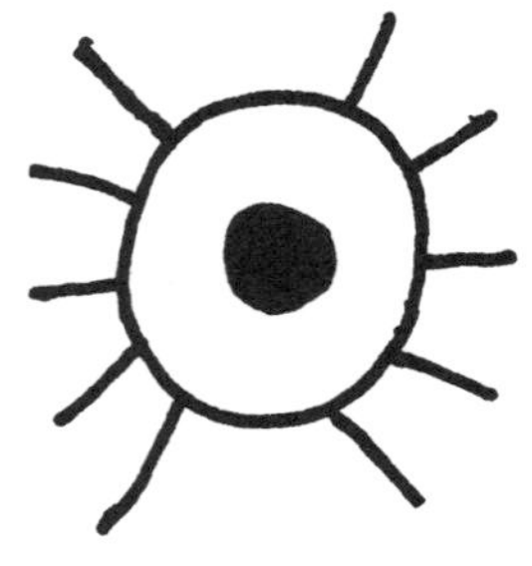

DIRECTIONS: Divide each of these amounts of money using your calculator. You may need to round the answer to the nearest cent. (To decide how to round your answer, look at the digit to the right of the cents place.) An example has been done for you.

EXAMPLE: $32.98 ÷ 19 = 1.735894 = $1.74

(number to the right of the cents place)

1. $46.75 ÷ 18 = H
2. $1.45 ÷ 27 = S
3. $65.32 ÷ 44 = T
4. $7.77 ÷ 12 = G
5. $0.56 ÷ 13 = L
6. $98.35 ÷ 38 = Y
7. $108.65 ÷ 45 = W
8. $32.77 ÷ 11 = A
9. $10.14 ÷ 37 = E
10. $31.05 ÷ 45 = B
11. $56.23 ÷ 98 = I

$0.69--$2.98--$0.65--$0.27--$0.04

$2.41--$0.57--$1.48--$2.60

$0.27--$2.59--$0.27--$0.04--$2.98--$0.05--$2.60--$0.27--$0.05

NAME ______________________________

DIVISIBILITY TRICKS FOR 3 AND 11

Divisibility by 3

RULE: Add all the single digits in the number. If the sum of the digits in the original number is a 2-digit number, add the digits in the sum. If the final sum is 3, 6, or 9, then the original number can be divided by 3.

EXAMPLE: 406,482
(1) 4 + 0 + 6 + 4 + 8 + 2 = 24
(2) 2 + 4 = 6
(3) Since the final sum is 6, then 406,482 can be divided by 3.

DIRECTIONS: Using the divisibility rule for 3, complete the table. If the original number is divisible by 3, find the quotient.

Number	Divisible by 3?	Quotient
1. 60,782		
2. 33,369,126		
3. 180,438		
4. 1,843		
5. 41,634,289		
6. 604,392		
7. 643,789,426,531,734 (bonus)		

Divisibility by 11

RULE: Reading the number from left to right, alternate minus and plus signs between the digits of the number. The first sign must be a minus. If the digit sum is divisible by 11, then the original number is also divisible by 11.

EXAMPLE: 6,134,788
(1) 6 - 1 + 3 - 4 + 7 - 8 + 8 = 11
(2) Since the final sum is 11, then 6,134,788 is divisible by 11.

DIRECTIONS: Using the divisibility rule for 11, complete the table. If the original number is divisible by 11, find the quotient.

Number	Divisible by 11?	Quotient
1. 60,782		
2. 63,369,185		
3. 180,438		
4. 8,195		
5. 41,634,289		
6. 604,395		
7. 643,789,426,531,735 (bonus)		

NAME________________________

What happens when corn catches a cold?

DIRECTIONS: First, work out the average of each set of numbers below. Second, locate your answers in the code. Third, every time the answer occurs in the code, write the letter of that problem above it.

G = Average of 45, 28, and 23 =

S = Average of 51, 26, and 40 =

R = Average of 138, 135, 138, 132, and 122 =

I = Average of 45, 37, 18, 29, 36, and 51 =

C = Average of 36, 37, and 59 =

N = Average of 28, 36, 42, 53, 37, and 26 =

H = Average of 132, 136, 127, 130, and 125 =

T = Average of 10, 13, 7, 10, 13, 9, 10, and 8 =

A = Average of 7, 18, 4, 23, 92, and 12 =

E = Average of 55, 11, 78, 7, 24, and 35 =

36--10 32--35--10--39 26--37 35--26--133--26--44--130--35

NAME______________________________

Mathosaurus: What was I?

DIRECTIONS: First, work out the average of each set of numbers below. Second, locate your answers in the code. Third, every time the answer occurs in the code, write the letter of that problem above it. If the remainder is greater than or equal to 1/2 of the divisor, round your answer up to the nearest whole number.

FACTS: I was one of the best known of the duck-billed dinosaurs. The helmet shape appendage on top of my head was a complicated breathing-tube system. I stood mainly on my hind legs and had no front teeth. A grown man would have only come up to my knees. What was I?

A = Average of 678, 436, 9847 and 4632 =

S = Average of 1679, 4735, 98, 643 and 7890 =

O = Average of 8736, 6745, 9000, 604 and 80 =

H = Average of 16, 34, 204, 19, 714 and 12 =

R = Average of 8437, 9345, 606, 7802 and 2 =

Y = Average of 18, 19, 348, 2704, 826, 973 and 80 =

U = Average of 678, 983, 483 and 643 =

T = Average of 9847, 6403, 8251, 8162, 4356 and 789 =

C = Average of 5746, 3845 and 92,645 =

34079--5033--5238--710--6301--167--5033--3009--3898--697--5238--697--3009

NAME____________________

Why did the whale cross the ocean?

To find the solution to this question, follow these directions. First, work the problems below and find the answer in the answer column. The number in front of the answer tells you where to put the letter of the problem in the row of boxes at the bottom of the page. Work problems on another sheet of paper.

G = 38,216 ÷ 37 =
T = 56,283 ÷ 27 =
R = 75,936 ÷ 38 =
H = 81,485 ÷ 74 =
O = $654.32 ÷ 39 =
D = 32,269 ÷ 23 =
T = 60,102 ÷ 81 =
O = 21,660 ÷ 57 =
H = 59,611 ÷ 93 =
E = $496.73 ÷ 47 =

I = 9284 ÷ 64 =
T = $859.73 ÷ 25 =
E = 74,555 ÷ 59 =
T = $946.74 ÷ 15 =
E = 22,706 ÷ 27 =
T = 92,307 ÷ 48 =
O = $782.98 ÷ 32 =
T = 35,537 ÷ 64 =
E = 15,984 ÷ 39 =

1. 742
2. $16.78
3. 1032 R32
4. $10.57
5. 2084 R15
6. $34.39
7. 380
8. $63.12
9. 1101 R11
10. 840 R26
11. $24.46
12. 555 R17
13. 640 R91
14. 409 R33
15. 1998 R12
16. 1923 R3
17. 145 R4
18. 1403
19. 1263 R38

1	2	3	4	5	6	7	8	9	10	11	12	13	14	15	16	17	18	19

NAME________________________

What does an octopus wear?

To find the solution to this question, follow these directions. First, work the problems below and find the answer in the answer column. The number in front of the answer tells you where to put the letter of the problem in the row of boxes at the bottom of the page. Work problems on another sheet of paper.

T = 8005 ÷ 65 =

M = 5921 ÷ 58 =

S = 3748 ÷ 18 =

R = 1710 ÷ 95 =

A = 4788 ÷ 84 =

C = 6508 ÷ 70 =

F = 7821 ÷ 23 =

O = 6413 ÷ 49 =

A = 60058 ÷ 76 =

O = 93774 ÷ 95 =

A = 35214 ÷ 84 =

1. 790 R18
2. 92 R68
3. 987 R9
4. 57
5. 123 R10
6. 130 R43
7. 340 R1
8. 419 R18
9. 18
10. 102 R5
11. 208 R4

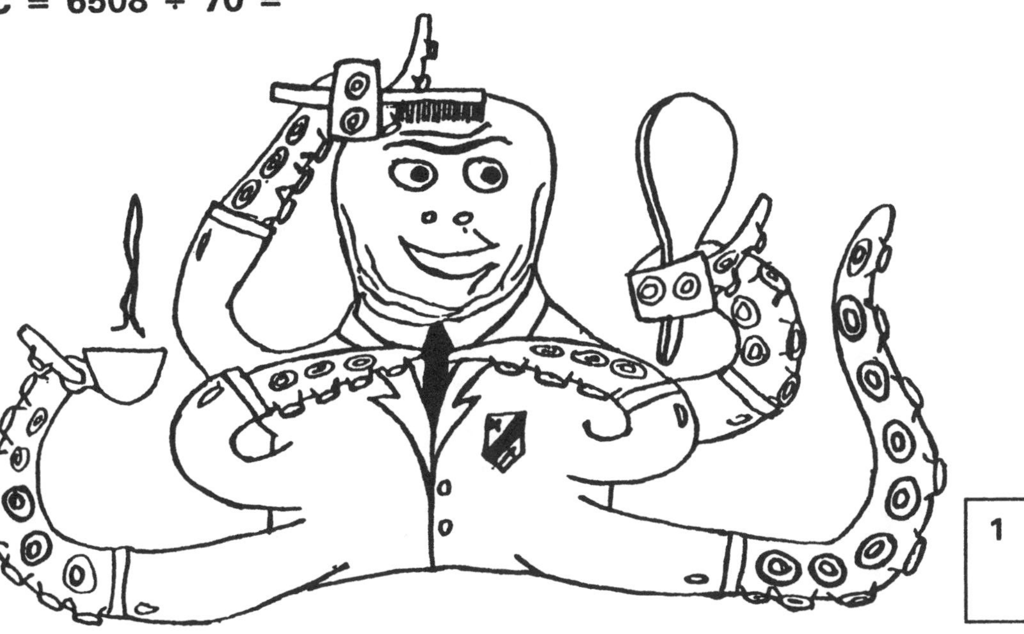

1	2	3	4	5	6	7	8	9	10	11

Dividing by two or three digit divisors

NAME____________________________

DIRECTIONS: Solve all the problems in Section 1 on another sheet of paper. Then circle the correct answers in the boxes in Section 2. Go on to Section 3 and connect the dots in the order of the boxes 1, 2, 3....22. To find the solution to the "Knock, Knock" riddle, place the letter from each "dot-to-dot" math problem answer into the same box in Section 2 as that answer.

1. Solve these problems:

160,371 ÷ 309 =	740,700 ÷ 900 =	27,720 ÷ 693 =
102,660 ÷ 236 =	59,760 ÷ 747 =	76,986 ÷ 91 =
45,625 ÷ 73 =	26,471 ÷ 103 =	33,480 ÷ 60 =
19,840 ÷ 320 =	184,864 ÷ 848 =	90,240 ÷ 384 =
9792 ÷ 288 =	45,625 ÷ 73 =	16,625 ÷ 475 =
420,452 ÷ 818 =	247,200 ÷ 600 =	45,000 ÷ 900 =
45,298 ÷ 58 =	58,520 ÷ 70 =	35,520 ÷ 64 =
		39,621 ÷ 47 =

KNOCK, KNOCK
WHO'S THERE?
SOUP!
SOUP WHO?

2. Circle your answer here in the correct box.

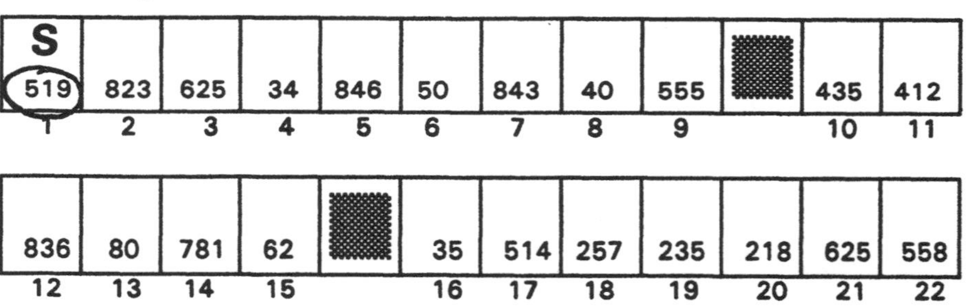

S									■		
519	823	625	34	846	50	843	40	555		435	412
1	2	3	4	5	6	7	8	9		10	11

				■							
836	80	781	62		35	514	257	235	218	625	558
12	13	14	15		16	17	18	19	20	21	22

3. Connect the dots in the order of the boxes above 1, 2, 3....22. Then place the letter beside each dot into the correct boxes above to make sure the letter goes into the same box above as the number beside each dot.

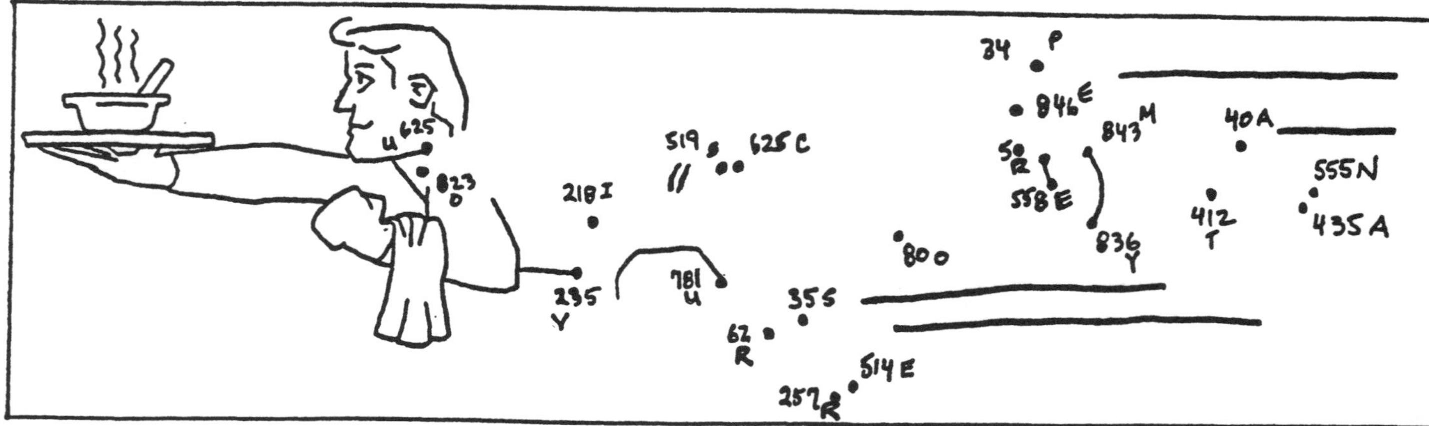

NAME______________________

What did the new tire say to the old tire?

DIRECTIONS: First, solve each problem below on a separate sheet of paper. Second, find your answer in the secret code at the bottom of the page. Third, each time your answer appears in the secret code, write the letter of the problem above it.

C = 48,122 ÷ 70 =

R = 56,102 ÷ 80 =

E = 36,080 ÷ 4 =

Y = 48,800 ÷ 96 =

N = 20,274 ÷ 31 =

O = 39,766 ÷ 835 =

F = 17,464 ÷ 236 =

A = 79,800 ÷ 700 =

D = 32,275 ÷ 374 =

I = 29,140 ÷ 432 =

T = 129,378 ÷ 976 =

U = 42,003 ÷ 300 =

67 R196--74   508 R32--47 R521--173 R103   687 R32--114--654--'132 R546

701 R22--9020--132 R546--701 R22--9020---114--86 R111,

701 R22--7020--132 R546--67 R196--701 R22--9020

Mixed whole number practice

NAME ______________________

Math Bingo

DIRECTIONS: Find the Math Bingo. Work all the problems below on a separate sheet of paper. Circle the correct answers in the puzzle. When you have five answers circled vertically, horizontally or diagonally, you have a Math Bingo. Draw a line through your Math Bingo to show you have solved the puzzle.

498	575,885	209	58	1208
16	307,402	26	514	10
105 R15	436	FREE SPACE	9642	69
97	1525	104	227,440	68
1048	18	1618	115	1008

1. 3 x (58-35) =
2. (2000 ÷ 4) - 2 =
3. 5436 ÷ 302 =
4. 3865 x 149 =
5. (122-99) x 5 =
6. (258 + 367) - 189 =
7. 1024 - (512 ÷ 32) =
8. 6315 ÷ 60 =
9. (26 ÷ 13) x 13 =
10. 942 + (365 + 218) =
11. 2843 x 80 =
12. (238x5) + 18 =
13. 48,540 ÷ 30 =
14. (6000 + 960) ÷ 120 =
15. (6356 ÷ 7) - 804 =
16. (144 ÷ 12) - 2 =
17. 2 x (918 ÷ 27) =

NAME________________________

What is a computer's favorite snack food?

DIRECTIONS: First, solve each problem below on a separate sheet of paper. Second, find your answer in the secret code at the bottom of the page. Third, each time your answer appears in the secret code, write the letter of the problem above it.

P = 6435 + (7892 - 3465) + (70,000 - 3463) =

H = (98,346 - 71,482) + (39,642 - 10,678) =

L = (61 x 934) + (7136 ÷ 32) - 6543 =

O = 238 x (1932 ÷ 28) =

N = (4144 ÷ 74) + (79,346 - 3425) =

C = (859 x 357) - (642 x 234) + 375 =

I = (32,121 ÷ 83) + (6 x 300) + 47,362 =

S = (783 x 436) + (52,004 - 24,685) x 3 =

1,106,121--49,549--50,654--49,549--156,810--16,422--75,977

156,810--55,828--49,549--77,399--1,106,121

NAME ____________________

Hexagonal Mania

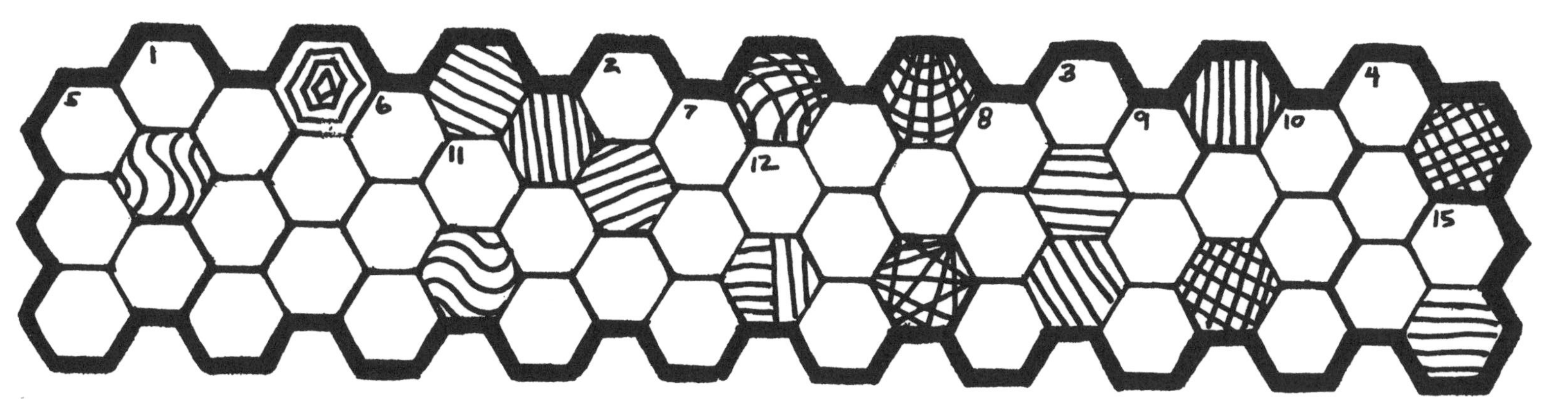

DIRECTIONS: Solve each problem and place your answer in the appropriate hexagon.

4. 10 x 10 = ________
5. 6 x 32 = ________
6. 493 + 381 = ________
7. 3408 ÷ 4 = ________
8. 3782 - 2961 = ________
9. (72 ÷ 6) x 12 = ________
10. (39 x 8) - 112 = ________
13. 8 x 8 x 8 = ________

1. 4095 - 2138 = ________
2. 6476 - 3675 = ________
3. 62,200 ÷ 2 = ________
6. 162,684 ÷ 2 = ________
10. (88 ÷ 11) x 19 = ________
13. 3072 ÷ 6 = ________

4. 6070 ÷ 5 = ________
6. 156,987 - 71,345 = ________
11. 8960 ÷ 5 = ________
13. 5054 x 10 = ________
15. 9000 ÷ 10 = ________

NAME______________________

Mathosaurus: What was I?

DIRECTIONS: First, work out the average of each set of numbers below. Second, locate your answers in the code. Third, every time the answer occurs in the code, write the letter of that problem above it. If the remainder is greater than or equal to 1/2 of the divisor, round your answer up to the nearest whole number.

FACTS: I was the second dinosaur to be named. My spike-like thumb was used as a weapon. I had no teeth but instead a bony beaklike mouth. What was I?

D = (43,321 - 5863) - (6472 - 2163) + 5821 =

U = (38,421 - 27,943) + (48,438 ÷ 26) =

N = 375 x (6018 ÷ 17) =

A = (398 x 256) - (66,720 - 22,763) + (476 x 8) =

O = (48,716 ÷ 641) x (78,106 ÷ 797) =

G = (58,642 - 33,782) - (13,548 + 10,794) x 6 =

I = 79 x (263,424 ÷ 2688) =

7742--3108--12,341--61,739--132,750--7448--38,970--7448--132,750

NAME________________________

Mixed whole number problem solving

What has sharp teeth, chops down cherry trees, and never tells lies?

DIRECTIONS: To find the answer to the riddle, solve each of the problems and locate your answer in the decoder. Each of the problems require only <u>one</u> operation to solve. Work your problems on another sheet of paper.

1. A soccer player ran 140 miles in 10 days as part of his preseason training. How many miles did he average each day? ______ = G
2. There are 168 onion plants in 7 boxes. How many plants are in each box? ________ = N
3. There are 150 gymnasts at a day camp. Each group has 15 gymnasts assigned to a coach. How many groups are at camp? ________ = I
4. There are 84 watermelon seeds and 7 seeds are planted in each hill. How many hills are needed for the seeds? ________ = A
5. One dozen doughnuts cost $1.56. What is the price of 1 doughnut? ________ = T
6. The 29 students in Mrs. Spiller's class gave $24.65 to Greenpeace to help save the whale. What was the average contribution from each student? ________ = W
7. One-half dozen large pickles cost $2.40. What is the price of one pickle? ________ = O
8. A window washer had 750 windows of a large office building to wash. He had 5 days to complete his job. How many windows must he average washing each day? ________ = S
9. How many days are in 720 hours? ________ = J
10. How many feet are in 540 inches? ________ = H

30--12--85--150

85--12--150--45--10--24--14--13--40--24

NAME________________________

What kind of gum do whales chew?

DIRECTIONS: Solve each of the division word problems and locate your answer in the decoder. Each time the answer appears in the secret code, write the letter in that problem above it. Some of these problems may require more than one mathematical operation.

1. Sally, Meg, and Meca decided to share the expense of a camping trip. They bought 2 lanterns at $12.50 each, 1 camping stove for $25.00, and a large water jug for $7.30. What was each girl's share of the expense for the camping items? ________ = G
2. A basketball player's points for eight games were 24, 18, 17, 12, 20, 14, 12, and 19. What was his average for the eight games? ________ = L
3. Chris and Mark decided to earn money by mowing lawns after school. On Monday they earned $12.30, Tuesday $10.50, Thursday $15.00, and on Friday $13.70. How much did each boy earn at the end of the week? ________ = E
4. The Keller family had seven days to get from Atlanta, Georgia to San Francisco, California. Using their map, they calculated the trip to be approximately 2,800 miles. How many miles will the Kellers need to average per day? ________ = R
5. Ryan wanted to buy 1 basketball and basketballs were on sale 2 for $24.40. If he gave the clerk $20.00, how much change should he receive? ________ = U
6. The Appalachian Trail begins in Georgia and ends in Maine. It is 2,000 miles long. If a hiker walked 25 miles a day, how many days would it take her to hike the trail? ________ = M
7. Bobby has published 6 newspapers for his fifth grade class. He worked 5 hours on his first paper, 4 on his second, 8 on his third, 3 on his fourth, 7 on his fifth and 9 on his sixth. How many hours did Bobby average working on each paper? ________ = B

6--17--$7.80--6--6--$25.75--400

$19.10--$7.80--80

NAME________________________

What kind of fish do knights eat?

DIRECTIONS: To find the answer to the riddle, solve each of the problems and locate your answer in the decoder. Work your problems on another sheet of paper.

1. Baseball star Hank Aaron holds the record as the private citizen who received the most personal letters in a year. He received 900,000 pieces of mail in June 1974 when he broke Babe Ruth's career home run record. How many letters did Aaron average receiving per day in the month of June? ________ = I

2. The largest king cobra ever recorded grew to be about 61 yards long. How many feet long was this cobra? ________ = R

3. The golden eagle can spot a hare about 2,150 yards away. How many feet are in 2150 yards? ________ = D

4. Brachiosaurus was probably the heaviest of all prehistoric animals. It is calculated that this reptile weighed at least 87 tons. How many pounds did this dinosaur weigh? ________ = W

5. A male African gray parrot named Purdle holds the world record for the largest vocabulary. In 11 years he has mastered almost 1000 words. On an average how many words per year did Purdle learn? ________ = H

6. An albatross can fly for 6 days without moving its wings because it can glide on air currents, has more feathers than most birds and is shaped for flying. How many hours can an albatross go without moving its wings? ________ = O

7. If it takes 12 men to hold down a python what would be the total number of men it would take to hold down 15 pythons? ________ = F

8. If a spider can weave at the rate of 1000 operations in a minute and it takes 20 minutes to create a whole web, at this rate how many operations are performed by a spider to complete a web? _______ = S

20,000--174,000--144--183--6450--180--30,000--20,000--91

NAME ______________________

What did the boy say when he opened his piggy bank and found nothing?

DIRECTIONS: To find the answer to the riddle, solve each of the problems and locate your answer in the decoder. Work your problems on another sheet of paper.

1. In the late 1800's over 40,000 tigers roamed wild in India. Today there are only 2,000 tigers living in India. How many more tigers were there in the late 1800's than there are today? _______ = T

2. The largest of all rhinoceroses is the almost extinct white rhinoceros. It weighs 3-1/2 tons and has a horn over 5 feet long. How many pounds does this rhinoceros weigh? _______ = M

3. In the 1600's beaver skins were very valuable. In fact, 12 of them could be traded for a rifle. How many rifles could be traded for 1,140 beaver skins? _______ = O

4. The pouch of a pelican can stretch so much that it can carry 30 pounds of fish. How many total fish could 25 pelicans carry if each carries 30 pounds of fish? _______ = U

5. The whistling swan has the most feathers of any bird with 25,216 and the humming bird has the least with 940. How many more feathers does the whistling swan have than the hummingbird? _______ = C

6. Great clams may weigh up to 500 pounds with their shells having a diameter of 4 feet. How much would 85 such clams weigh? _______ = I

7. The ostrich, the largest bird in the world has an amazing ability to run. This remarkable animal can reach up to speeds of 60 miles per hour when trying to escape from a predator. In one stride, it can cover 25 feet. At that pace, how many strides has an ostrich taken if it has covered a distance of 1,250 feet? _______ = R

95 42,500 24,276 750 50 7,000 38,000

NAME________________________

What invention allows you to see through walls?

DIRECTIONS: To find the answer to the riddle, solve each of the problems and locate your answer in the decoder. Work your problems on another sheet of paper.

1. Each of 6 boys bought 38 coins to a school hobby show. How many coins did the 6 boys bring in all? _______ = O

2. The moon revolves around our Earth at the speed of 88,800 kilometers in 24 hours. How many total kilometers does it travel in 3 days? _______ = N

3. Brontosaurus, the thunder lizard, had a tiny head that contained a brain that was about as large as a man's fist. However, this dinosaur's total weight was 33 tons. How many pounds did Brontosaurus weigh? _______ = D

4. Leah scored 9 goals her first season in soccer, 12 her second season, 11 her third season and 16 goals her fourth season. What was Leah's average for the four seasons she played? _______ = I

5. There are 24 cans of tomato soup in each of 12 boxes and 20 cans of onion soup in each of 13 boxes. How many cans of soup are there in all? _______ = A

6. Amy purchased 2 sweaters at $10.95 each, 1 pair of socks for $2.50, 1 pair of jeans for $16.95 and 3 pairs of earrings at $1.95 each. How much change should she receive from a $50 bill? _______ = W

548 $2.80--12--266,400--66,000--228--$2.80

DIVISION FACTS SPEED TEST

NAME ____________________

DATE ____________________

SCORE ____________________
(88 Facts)

12 ÷ 3 =	2 ÷ 2 =	0 ÷ 7 =	56 ÷ 8 =
64 ÷ 8 =	28 ÷ 7 =	18 ÷ 3 =	30 ÷ 6 =
63 ÷ 9 =	56 ÷ 7 =	8 ÷ 2 =	16 ÷ 8 =
0 ÷ 2 =	20 ÷ 4 =	63 ÷ 7 =	0 ÷ 9 =
18 ÷ 6 =	1 ÷ 1 =	4 ÷ 2 =	35 ÷ 7 =
12 ÷ 2 =	21 ÷ 7 =	8 ÷ 8 =	16 ÷ 4 =
5 ÷ 1 =	72 ÷ 9 =	2 ÷ 1 =	24 ÷ 8 =
18 ÷ 9 =	72 ÷ 8 =	0 ÷ 1 =	40 ÷ 8 =
35 ÷ 5 =	6 ÷ 2 =	48 ÷ 6 =	42 ÷ 6 =
14 ÷ 7 =	24 ÷ 3 =	7 ÷ 1 =	81 ÷ 9 =
24 ÷ 6 =	0 ÷ 4 =	3 ÷ 1 =	25 ÷ 5 =
8 ÷ 4 =	3 ÷ 3 =	15 ÷ 3 =	36 ÷ 6 =
27 ÷ 9 =	54 ÷ 6 =	21 ÷ 3 =	12 ÷ 4 =
15 ÷ 5 =	4 ÷ 4 =	8 ÷ 1 =	36 ÷ 4 =
16 ÷ 2 =	10 ÷ 2 =	14 ÷ 2 =	6 ÷ 3 =
18 ÷ 2 =	49 ÷ 7 =	0 ÷ 3 =	0 ÷ 8 =
0 ÷ 5 =	9 ÷ 1 =	40 ÷ 5 =	9 ÷ 9 =
28 ÷ 4 =	12 ÷ 6 =	10 ÷ 5 =	45 ÷ 9 =
7 ÷ 7 =	6 ÷ 1 =	27 ÷ 3 =	20 ÷ 5 =
48 ÷ 8 =	32 ÷ 8 =	45 ÷ 5 =	54 ÷ 9 =
24 ÷ 4 =	9 ÷ 3 =	36 ÷ 9 =	
6 ÷ 6 =	32 ÷ 4 =	5 ÷ 5 =	
42 ÷ 7 =	30 ÷ 5 =		

Movin' On

BRAIN CHALLENGERS:

MULTIPLICATION AND DIVISION

NAME______________________________

Shared Sides

DIRECTIONS: Using the numbers 2 through 9 for both boxes without using any number more than once in each box, fill in the white squares with numbers so that their sum equals the number in the shaded square touching them.

EXAMPLE:

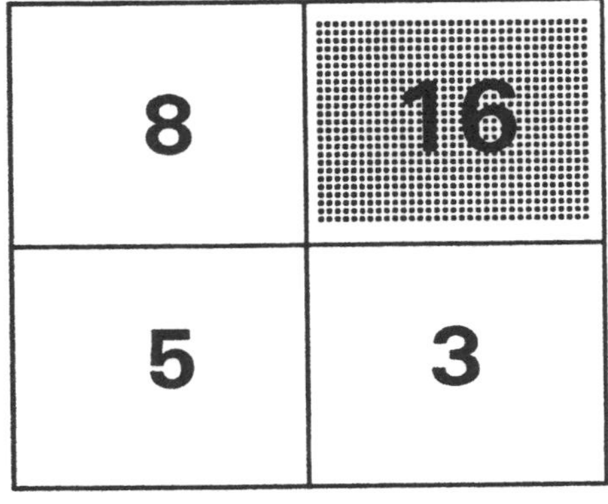

8 + 5 + 3 = 16

	18		13
16		18	
	14		17
9		15	

2 3 4 5 6 7 8 9

	18		11
13		19	
	16		18
8		20	

2 3 4 5 6 7 8 9

NAME______________________________

Maze Math

DIRECTIONS: Start at the top line and move to the bottom line. You may move vertically, diagonally or horizontally.

EXAMPLE: Move through this maze making the total 300 by multiplying each number by the next.

3	5	7	10	1	8
9	1	6	9	9	4
8	2	4	1	6	7
2	8	1	4	5	8

EXAMPLE:

3 x 5 = 15 x 1 =

15 x 4 = 60 x 1 =

60 x 5 = 300

Move through this maze making the total 192 by multiplying each number by the next.

6	2	1	8	4	7
8	6	4	2	1	2
1	3	3	2	5	3
7	9	2	6	4	1

1	2	3	5	3	4
4	1	6	2	2	3
3	6	2	9	6	1
7	4	5	1	8	5
5	8	2	4	3	1
2	1	9	3	5	7

Move through this maze making the total 192 by multiplying each number by the next.

Move through this maze making the total 360 by multiplying each number by the next.

1	2	3	5	3	4
4	1	6	2	2	3
3	6	2	9	6	1
7	4	5	1	8	5
5	8	2	4	3	1
2	1	9	3	5	7

NAME________________________________

Operational Choices

DIRECTIONS: Place all the numbers below on the chart to make 8 number sentences.

9 1 11 5 6

3 4 2 4 2

20 7 3 1 3

18

	x		+		=	
x		+		–		+
	+		x		=	
–		–		x		–
	+		x		=	
=		=		=		=
	x		–		=	

Analysis and synthesis

NAME ______________________

Using Whole Numbers with Geometry

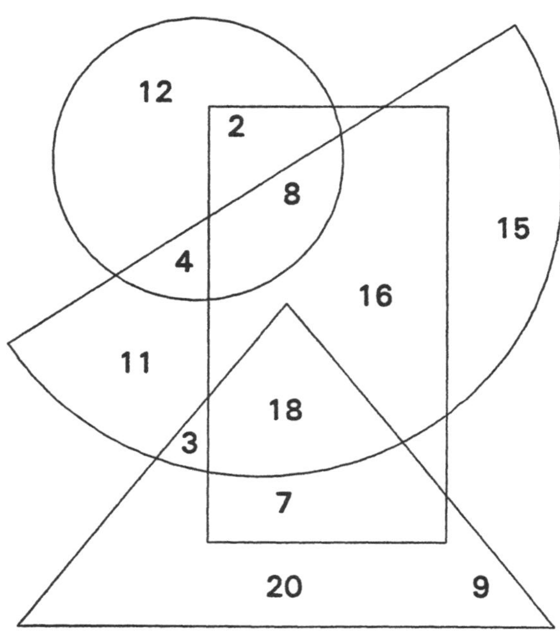

1. What shape has the fewest numbers?
____

2. What shape has the most numbers?
____

3. What shapes are the "8" part of?
____

4. What is the sum of the numbers in the triangle but not in the rectangle? __________

5. What is the largest number in the rectangle but not in the half circle? __________

6. What is the smallest number in the circle but not in the half circle? __________

7. Multiply the only number found in the triangle, the rectangle, and the half circle by the number found only in the circle. __________

8. What number lies outside the rectangle but is within both the circle and the half circle? __________

9. What is the sum of the numbers in the triangle? __________

10. What would the answer be if you multiplied the number found only in the triangle and half circle but not in the rectangle by the number found in the half circle and rectangle but in no other space?
____

11. What number in the triangle is part of the rectangle but no other space? __________

12. Multiply the number found only in the circle by the number found in the circle, half circle, and rectangle.
____

13. What is the sum of the numbers found in only one shape? __________

14. What shape has the largest number sum within?
____

15. What is the sum of all the numbers? __________

NAME________________________

Fill In The Missing Digits

DIRECTIONS: Find the correct number for each blank to make the number sentences true. Some have more than one solution. You need to multiply and divide before you add or subtract!

1. 15 ÷ ____ + ____ x 6 = 35
2. ____ x ____ + 55 = 80
3. 20 ÷ ____ + 3 x ____ = 28
4. 175 ÷ ____ – ____ x 4 = 15
5. 4 x ____ ÷ ____ = 8
6. 33 – ____ + 64 ÷ ____ = 19
7. ____ x 5 ÷ 3 = 100
8. 136 ÷ ____ – ____ = 60
9. ____ x 12 + 2 x ____ = 200
10. 8 x ____ ÷ ____ = 4
11. ____ ÷ 3 + 3 x ____ = 60
12. ____ ÷ 5 + ____ = 75

NAME________________________

"30" Math

DIRECTIONS: By adding, subtracting, multiplying, or dividing, make the following sets of 4 numbers equal 30!

EXAMPLE:

	1	
6		7
	5	

5 x 7 = 35 - 6 = 29 + 1 = 30

1.

	9	
8		3
	5	

2.

	3	
4		6
	3	

3.

	6	
9		2
	3	

4.

	7	
6		4
	8	

5.

	9	
5		3
	2	

6.

	8	
2		2
	8	

NAME____________________

Box Equations

DIRECTIONS: Place all the numbers below in the box to form eight equations.

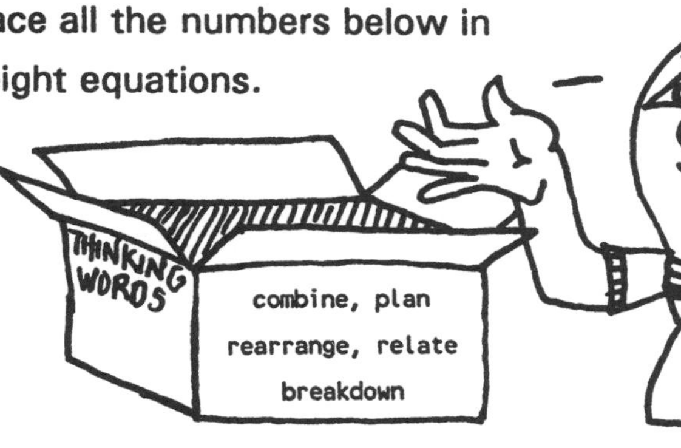

	x		—		=	
+		+		+		+
	+		—		=	
—		÷		+		—
	+		+		=	
=		=		=		=
	—		+		=	

6	8	14	9	4	2	11	13
3	10	5	2	1	4	6	2

NAME ______________________________

Puzzlers

DIRECTIONS: Using addition and multiplication only, solve the following problems. If both multiplication and addition are used, multiplication should be used first.

EXAMPLE: Use 5 3's to make 13

$3 \times 3 = 9 + 3 = 12 + \frac{3}{3} = 13$

HIGHER LEVEL THINKING

THINKING WORDS
order
separate
combine
predict

1. Use 3 6's to make 42
2. Use 4 4's to make 17
3. Use 5 5's to make 6
4. Use 4 7's to make 49
5. Use 4 2's and 1 3 to make 50
6. Use 8 1's to make 33
7. Use 2 6's and 3 2's to make 50
8. Use 10 1's to make 5
9. Use 4 2's to make 88
10. Use 2 3's and 3 1's to make 35

(You may use only the numbers given and no others! Be creative with your solutions!)

NAME________________________

School Lunch Menu

The cafeteria supervisor wanted to make a special breakfast on the first day of school for the 200 students at Learnwell Elementary. She wanted to serve Spicy Sausage/Egg Casserole, and Coffee Cake Supreme.

Spicy Sausage/Egg Casserole
(serves 10)

1 c. butter

1 lb. sausage

6 eggs

1 c. milk

2 tsp. salt

2 c. flour

Coffee Cake Supreme
(serves 5)

3 c. flour

1 c. sugar

2 c. milk

3 eggs

1 c. butter

1/2 tsp. vanilla

1 tsp. salt

1/2 tsp. cinnamon

How much of the following ingredients will she have to buy?

1. ____________ doz. eggs
2. ____________ c. flour
3. ____________ c. milk
4. ____________ c. butter
5. ____________ tsp. salt

Application and analysis

NAME______________________

FIND THE SUM

DIRECTIONS: Find the 5 cherries that add up to 79 and place the numbers in the cherries on the cone.

DIRECTIONS: Find the 4 donuts that add up to 63 and place the numbers on the stacked donuts.

DIRECTIONS: Find the 4 apples that add up to 86 and place the numbers in the apples on the tree.

DIRECTIONS: Find the 5 flowers that add up to 116 and place the numbers in the flowers in the basket.

NAME______________________________

Shape Math

DIRECTIONS: Replace shapes with numbers that make the math problems true. Use the numbers 1-9 to solve. Each problem has a <u>different</u> code.

1.

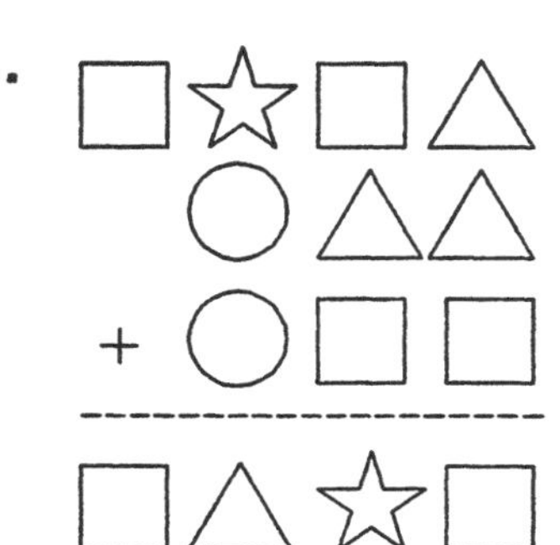

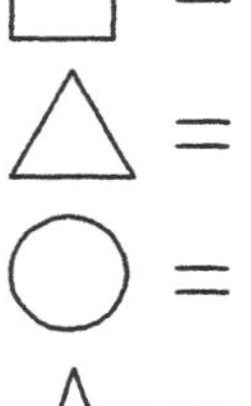

2.

3.

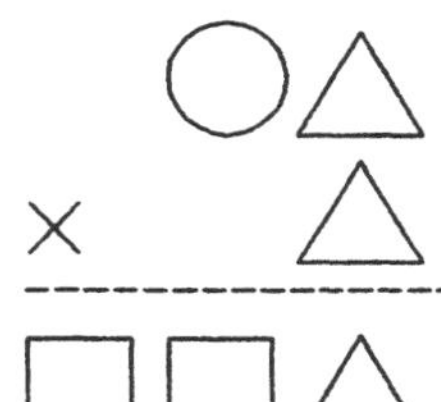

4.

5.

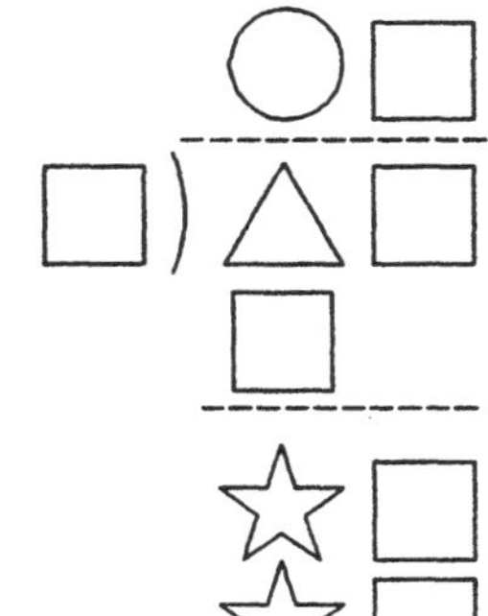

NAME________________________________

Math Squares

DIRECTIONS FOR THE THREE SQUARE: Using the numbers 5, 10, 15, 20, 25, 30, 35, 40 and 45, fill in the 3 by 3 square so that each row, each column, and both diagonals add up to 75!

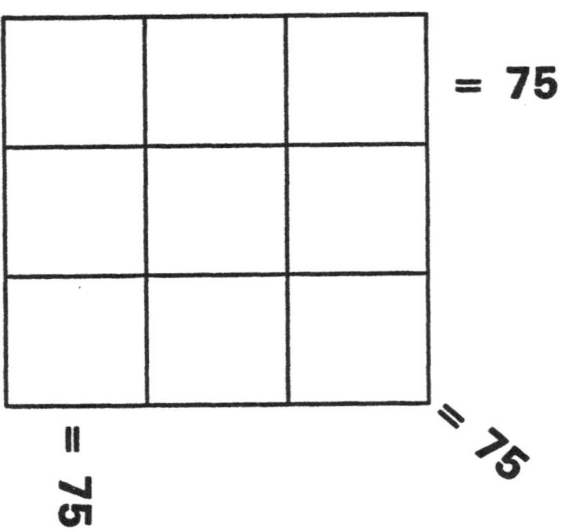

DIRECTIONS FOR THE FOUR SQUARE: Using the odd numbers from 1 to 31 (1, 3, 5, 7, ...), fill in the 4 by 4 square so that each row, column, and both diagonals add up to 64.

= 64

= 64

= 64

NAME______________________________

Operation Solutions

DIRECTIONS: To solve these problems, use the mathematical operations that are given. You will need to multiply and divide before you add and subtract. Numbers may be grouped, but the order may not be rearranged. No parentheses are needed. An example has been done for you.

EXAMPLE:

Use one (−) and one (+) sign:

4 3 2 8 = 49

43 − 2 + 8 = 49

1. Use one (+) and one (x) sign: 9 7 3 = 30
2. Use two (+) and two (÷) signs: 1 2 4 5 6 3 = 10
3. Use one (+) and one (−) sign: 6 4 2 3 2 = 16
4. Use one (+), one (÷), and one (x) sign: 1 0 2 0 5 4 = 26
5. Use one (x), one (+), and one (+) sign: 1 0 5 5 2 2 5 = 67
6. Use one (+), one (−), and one (+) sign: 1 6 8 4 2 1 2 = 32
7. Use two (+) and two (−) signs: 8 6 2 4 4 2 = 24
8. Use one (+) and two (−) signs: 4 2 4 1 2 4 = 15
9. Use two (+) and one (−) sign: 3 2 1 3 2 1 = 6
10. Use one (−) and one (+) sign: 1 2 6 4 3 2 = 10
11. Use two (−), one (x), and two (+) signs: 2 4 1 2 6 3 2 1 = 13
12. Use two (+) and two (−) signs: 9 3 6 2 3 1 = 41

NAME ____________________

Circular Math Magic

DIRECTIONS: A long-used math trick called circular math has mystified many people over the years. Your job is to explain why it works! The last answer is always the number you started with!

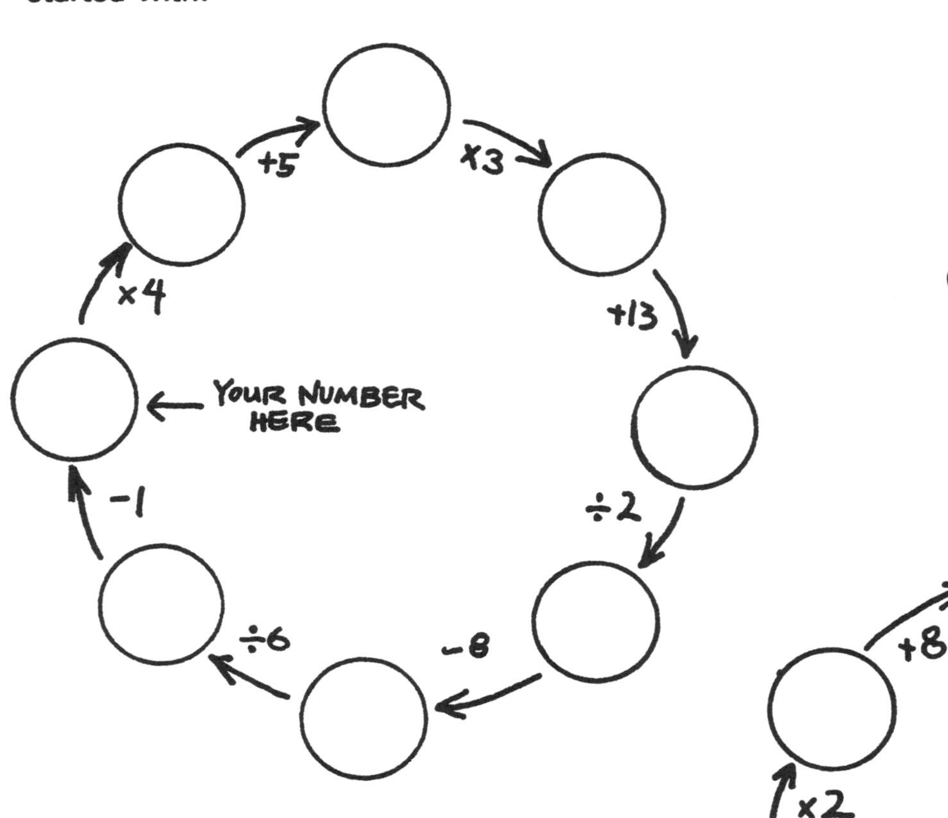

Circular math works because ____

____

____

____

NAME________________________________

Math Patterns

DIRECTIONS: Find the pattern and fill in the missing numbers.
(Some are easy and some are very difficult.)

1. 1, 2, 5, 10, 17, ____, ____, ____

2. 2, 2, 4, 6, 10, 16, ____, ____, ____

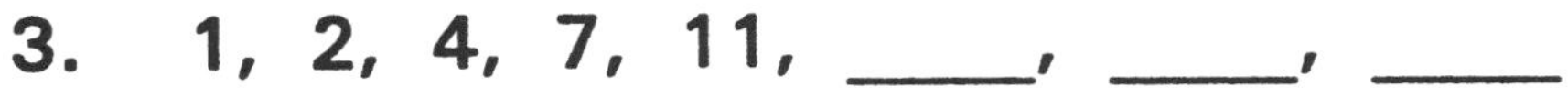

3. 1, 2, 4, 7, 11, ____, ____, ____

4. 52, 47, 42, 37, ____, ____, ____

5. 1, 2, 4, 7, 12, 19, ____, ____, ____

6. 1, 3, 7, 13, 21, ____, ____, ____

7. 1, 43, 2, 41, 3, 39, 4, 37, ____, ____, ____

8. 2, 4, 9, 16, 25, ____, ____, ____

9. 11, 22, 66, 264, 1320, ____, ____, ____

10. 3, 5, 6, 10, 9, 15, 12, ____, ____, ____

NAME ______________________

How many ways can you make change?

DIRECTIONS: Change a one dollar bill into coins. There are 40 possible ways. See how many you can find! (No pennies allowed.)

	5¢	10¢	25¢	50¢
1.	___	___	___	___
2.	___	___	___	___
3.	___	___	___	___
4.	___	___	___	___
5.	___	___	___	___
6.	___	___	___	___
7.	___	___	___	___
8.	___	___	___	___
9.	___	___	___	___
10.	___	___	___	___
11.	___	___	___	___
12.	___	___	___	___
13.	___	___	___	___
14.	___	___	___	___
15.	___	___	___	___
16.	___	___	___	___
17.	___	___	___	___
18.	___	___	___	___
19.	___	___	___	___
20.	___	___	___	___

	5¢	10¢	25¢	50¢
21.	___	___	___	___
22.	___	___	___	___
23.	___	___	___	___
24.	___	___	___	___
25.	___	___	___	___
26.	___	___	___	___
27.	___	___	___	___
28.	___	___	___	___
29.	___	___	___	___
30.	___	___	___	___
31.	___	___	___	___
32.	___	___	___	___
33.	___	___	___	___
34.	___	___	___	___
35.	___	___	___	___
36.	___	___	___	___
37.	___	___	___	___
38.	___	___	___	___
39.	___	___	___	___
40.	___	___	___	___

NAME____________________

Honeycomb Math

DIRECTIONS: Shade in the number in the honeycomb that matches the description given in each of the statements below. An example has been done for you.

EXAMPLE: Find the "5" that when added to the six numbers touching it equals 39.

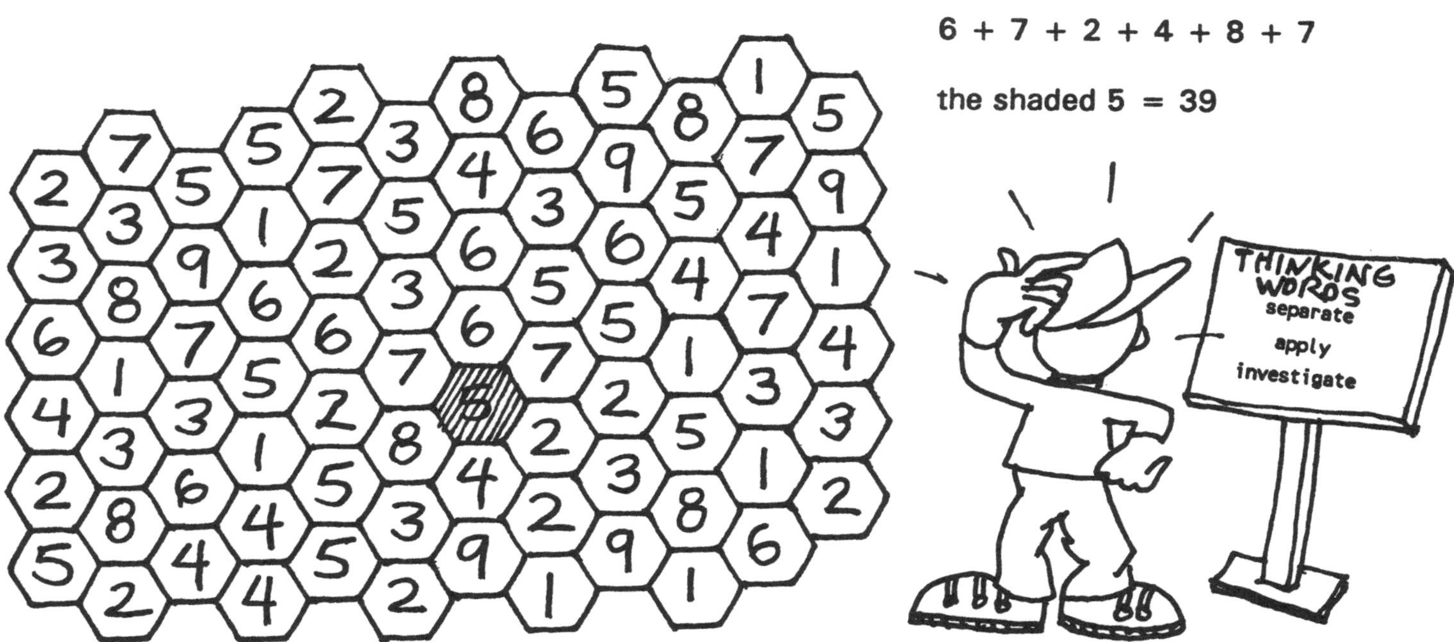

1. Find the "6" that when added to the six numbers touching it equals 36.

2. Find the "1" that when each of the six numbers touching it are multiplied by each other equals 4200.

3. Find the "3" that when added to the six numbers touching it equals 31.

4. Find the "2" that when each of the six numbers touching it are multiplied by each other and then by 2 equals 3360.

5. Find the "4" that when divided into the sum of the surrounding six numbers equals 7.

6. Find the "7" that when multiplied by the sum of the surrounding six numbers equals 126.

7. Find the "8" that when multiplied by the sum of the surrounding six numbers equals 208.

8. Find the "9" that when multiplied by the sum of the surrounding six numbers equals 270.

NAME ______________________

Letter Code

DIRECTIONS: The numbers have been replaced by letters! By studying the problems, can you find the code word?

___	___	___	___	___	___	___	___	___	___
0	1	2	3	4	5	6	7	8	9

```
     O S E
P ) P L B
    P
      L
      A
      S B
      S B
```

```
      A L E
I ) S B T A
    S I
      P T
      P S
        P A
        P A
```

```
     L A
I ) P I I
    P S
      S I
      S I
```

```
     T O
I ) S H I
    S H
        I
        I
```

```
   P T E
 - S E T
     A I
```

```
   E L E T
 -   P T E
   E T P A
```

HINT: P = 3 (Everywhere you see a "P", place a 3.)

NAME________________________________

Multiplication Stumpers

1. If a man and a half builds a boat and a half in a day and a half, how many boats will 7 men build in 6 days? (Hard!)

2. Four baseball teams were in a tournament. If each team plays each of the other teams, how many games will be played?

3. Mrs. Jones had quite a few puppies. All her puppies were either all black or all brown. If all the puppies were in a pen and the lights went out so Mrs. Jones couldn't see, how many puppies would she have to take out to be sure she got at least 2 all black puppies?

4. Bob loved chocolate covered cherries. He ate a total of 90 cherries over a period of 5 days. Each day he ate 4 more than the previous day. How many cherries did he eat on the first day?

ANSWER KEY

1. WHEN BIG CHIEF SHORTCAKE DIED WHAT DID HIS WIDOW SAY? Straw bury shortcake

2. WHAT DID THE PONY SAY WHEN HE SNEEZED? Excuse me, I am a little hoarse

3. WHY DID THE LADY HOLD HER EARS WHEN SHE WALKED PAST THE CHICKENS?
   Because she did not want to listen to their fowl language

4. WHAT HAS 18 LEGS AND CATCHES FLIES? A baseball team

5. WHY DID THE MAN IN JAIL WANT TO CATCH THE MEASLES? He wanted to break out

6. WHAT SICKNESS CAN'T YOU TALK ABOUT UNTIL IT'S CURED? The sickness laryngitis

7. MULTIPLES
   (2) 0, 7, 14, 21, 28, 35, 42, 49, 56, 63
   (3) 0, 5, 10, 15, 20, 25, 30, 35, 40, 45
   (4) 0, 12, 24, 36, 48, 60, 72, 84, 96, 108
   (5) 0, 2, 4, 6, 8, 10, 12, 14, 16, 18
   (6) 0, 4, 8, 12, 16, 20, 24, 28, 32, 36
   (7) 0, 9, 18, 27, 36, 45, 54, 63, 72, 81
   (8) 0, 10, 20, 30, 40, 50, 60, 70, 80, 90
   (9) 0, 8, 16, 24, 32, 40, 48, 56, 64, 72

   (11) 20; (12) 36; (13) 21; (14) 14; (15) 72; (16) 10; (17) 28; (18) 60; (19) 8; (20) 20; (21) 56

8. MULTIPLES, MULTIPLES, MULTIPLES
   1. 8: 8, 16, 24, 32, 40, 48, 56, 64, 72
   2. 12: 24, 36, 48, 60, 72, 84, 96, 108
   3. 16: 32, 48, 64, 80, 96, 112, 128, 144
   4. 13: 26, 39, 52, 65, 78, 91, 104, 117
   5. 25: 50, 75, 100, 125, 150, 175, 200, 225
   6. 125: 250, 375, 500, 625, 750, 875, 1000, 1125
   7. 14: 28, 42, 56, 70, 84, 98, 112, 126
   8. 18: 36, 54, 72, 90, 108, 126, 144, 162
   9. 15: 30, 45, 60, 75, 90, 105, 120, 135
   10. 38: 76, 114, 152, 190, 228, 266, 304, 342

9. WHAT DO YOU GET IF A DINOSAUR STEPS ON YOUR FOOT? You get anklesaurus

10-11. STATE IDENTIFICATION PUZZLE - EASTERN UNITED STATES

1935 = Missouri	2856 = Minnesota	6040 = Arkansas
5202 = Iowa	4193 = Alabama	2864 = Florida
4242 = Indiana	4080 = Maine	4698 = Connecticut
5664 = Illinois	2690 = Virginia	4203 = Georgia
372 = Louisiana	5936 = Pennsylvania	792 = South Carolina
3740 = Wisconsin	1479 = New York	5733 = New Jersey
1368 = West Virginia	3608 = Delaware	918 = Rhode Island
1809 = Kentucky	3228 = Mississippi	5614 = Vermont
3710 = Michigan	4810 = Massachusetts	5888 = Ohio
6400 = North Carolina	3140 = New Hampshire	1828 = Maryland
5940 = Tennessee		

12. HOW CAN YOU TELL A HAPPY MOTORCYCLIST? By the bugs in his teeth

13. WHAT DID THE CLOTHESLINE SAY TO THE WET LAUNDRY? Why don't you hang around awhile

14. KING TUT'S FACTOR PYRAMIDS - LEVEL 1

8	12	9	25	10	20	24	15
1x8	1x12	1x9	1x25	1x10	1x20	1x24	1x15
2x4	2x6	3x3	5x5	2x5	2x10	2x12	3x5
	3x4				x5	3x8	
						6x4	

16	18	30	27	32	40	28	50
1x16	1x18	1x30	1x27	1x32	1x40	1x28	1x50
4x4	2x9	5x6	3x9	2x16	8x5	2x14	2x25
2x8	3x6	2x15		4x8	2x20	4x7	5x10
		3x10			4x10		

15. KING TUT'S FACTOR PYRAMIDS - LEVEL 2

18	15	24	27	50	72	36	48
1x18	1x15	1x24	1x27	1x50	1x72	1x36	1x48
2x9	3x5	2x12	3x9	2x25	2x36	2x18	2x24
3x6		4x6		5x10	3x24	3x12	3x16
					4x18	4x9	4x12
					6x12	6x6	6x8
					8x9		

30	38	26	40	60	100	56	200
1x30	1x38	1x26	1x40	1x60	1x100	1x56	1x200
2x15	2x19	2x13	2x20	2x30	2x50	2x28	2x100
3x10			4x10	3x20	4x25	4x14	4x50
5x6			5x8	4x15	5x20	7x8	5x40
				5x12	10x10		8x25
				6x10			10x20

16. WHAT IS THE TITLE OF THIS PICTURE? A spider doing a handstand

17. WHAT DID NOAH USE TO SEE IN THE DARK? Floodlights

18. WHY IS TENNIS SUCH A NOISY GAME? Because each player raises a racket

19. WHAT DID ONE MATH BOOK SAY TO ANOTHER? Boy, do I have problems

20. WHAT'S 8 FEET TALL, PATRIOTIC AND FLIES KITES IN A RAINSTORM? Benjamin Frankenstein

21-22. STATE IDENTIFICATION PUZZLE - WESTERN UNITED STATES

9672 = Oklahoma	47,377 = New Mexico	22,752 = Utah
10,638 = Nebraska	45,372 = California	11,151 = Alaska
36,288 = Arizona	59,057 = North Dakota	50,853 = Washington
12,519 = Wyoming	31,941 = Colorado	11,607 = Montana
12,516 = Hawaii	51,402 = Nevada	11,970 = South Dakota
47,040 = Texas	43,818 = Oregon	4605 = Idaho
19,800 = Kansas		

23. WHY DID THE PRESIDENT OF THE UNITED STATES ARRANGE A MEETING WITH A CARPENTER? He wanted to replace his cabinet

24. WHAT HAPPENED WHEN THE MALE MONSTER MET THE FEMALE MONSTER? Love at first fright

25. WHAT'S THE DIFFERENCE BETWEEN A PIANO AND A FISH? You can tune a piano but you cannot tuna fish

26. WHAT DID THE BREAD DOUGH SAY TO THE BAKER? It's nice to be kneaded

27. WHY DID THE CHIMNEY CALL THE DOCTOR? Because the chimney had the flue

28. WHY DID THE NUCLEAR POWERED ROBOT BREAK DOWN? It had atomic ache

29. LATTICE MULTIPLICATION (1) 477,414 (2) 62,832 (3) 11,178 (4) 3,045,504 (5) 53,872,885
Super challenge: (A) 94,145,490 (B) 28,559,260,184

30. MULTIPLYING WITH A CALCULATOR
ACTIVITY ONE (1) 56 x 56 (2) 24 x 24 (3) 63 x 63 (4) 49 x 49 (5) 74 x 74
(6) 21 x 21 (7) 32 x 32 (8) 96 x 96 (9) 122 x 122

ACTIVITY TWO (1) 33,994 (2) 387,855 (3) 5,830,836 (4) 583,506 (5) 5,840,532

31. WHAT IS THE MINISTER DOING WHEN HE REHEARSES HIS SERMON? He is practicing what he preaches

32. WHERE DO MOLES GET MARRIED? In a tunnel of love

33. WHY DID THE DETECTIVE ARREST THE BASEBALL PLAYER? He heard that he stole a lot of bases

34. WHY SHOULDN'T YOU MENTION THE NUMBER 288 ALOUD IN FRONT OF THE PRINCIPAL? Because the number is two gross

36. WHERE DO POLAR BEARS VOTE? At the North Pole

37. WHAT DID ONE WALL SAY TO THE OTHER WALL? I will meet you at the corner

38. WHAT TIME DO DUCKS GET UP IN THE MORNING? At the quack of dawn

39. WHAT IS THE DIFFERENCE BETWEEN A DOG AND A MARINE BIOLOGIST? One wags a tail and the other tags a whale

40. WHAT KIND OF CAR DO RICH ROCK STARS DRIVE? A rock and rolls royce

41. WHAT DO YOU FIND ON A MOUSE'S CHEEK AFTER HE'S BEEN SPANKED? Mouse-ka-teers

42. WHAT DID THE PENCIL SAY TO THE PENCIL SHARPENER? Stop going around in circles and get to the point

43. WHY DID THE RAM FALL OVER THE CLIFF? He did not see the ewe turn

44. WHY DID THE HOUSE CALL FOR A DOCTOR? Because it had window panes

45. WHY DID THE BOWLING PINS LIE DOWN? Because they were on strike

46. DO RABBITS USE COMBS? No, they use hare brushes

47. WHY DID THE JOGGER GO SEE THE VETERINARIAN? Because his calves hurt

48. WHAT PLANTS ARE THE GREEDIEST? Weeds, give them an inch and they will take a yard

49. WHAT IS THE TITLE OF THIS PICTURE? Bagel with eyelashes

50. DIVISIBILITY TRICKS FOR 3 AND 11
DIVISIBILITY BY 3— (1) No (2) Yes 11,123,042 (3) Yes 60,146 (4) No (5) Yes 13,878,096 (6) Yes 201,464
(7) Yes 214,596,475,510,578 (bonus)

DIVISIBILITY BY 11— (1) Yes 8,729 (2) Yes 5,760,835 (3) No (4) Yes 745 (5) No (6) Yes 54,945
(7) Yes 58,526,311,502,885 (bonus)

51. WHAT HAPPENS WHEN CORN CATCHES A COLD? It gets an earache

52. MATHOSAURUS: WHAT WAS I? Corythosaurus

53. WHY DID THE WHALE CROSS THE OCEAN? To get to the other tide

54. WHAT DOES AN OCTOPUS WEAR? A coat of arms

55. KNOCK, KNOCK, WHO'S THERE? SOUP. SOUP WHO? Souperman at your service

519 = S	823 = O	40 = A
435 = A	80 = O	846 = E
625 = U	257 = R	558 = E
62 = R	218 = I	235 = V
34 = P	625 = C	35 = S
514 = E	412 = T	50 = R
781 = U	836 = Y	555 = N
		843 = M

56. WHAT DID THE NEW TIRE SAY TO THE OLD TIRE? If you can't retread, retire

57. MATH BINGO

1. 69
2. 498
3. 18
4. 575,885
5. 115
6. 436
7. 1008
8. 108 R15
9. 26
10. 1525
11. 227,440
12. 1208
13. 1618
14. 58
15. 104
16. 10
17. 68

58. WHAT IS A COMPUTER'S FAVORITE SNACK FOOD? Silicon chips

59. HEXAGONAL MANIA

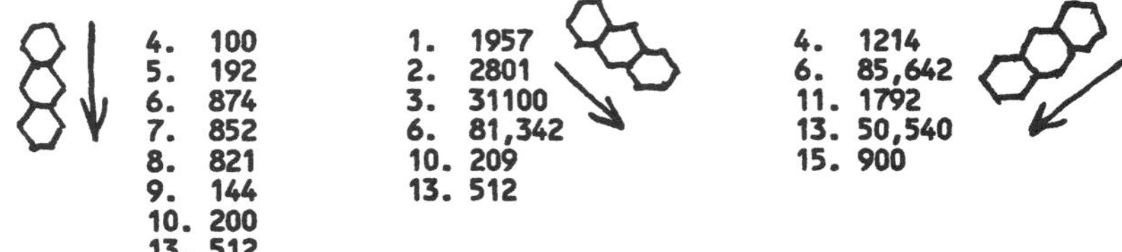

4. 100
5. 192
6. 874
7. 852
8. 821
9. 144
10. 200
13. 512

1. 1957
2. 2801
3. 31100
6. 81,342
10. 209
13. 512

4. 1214
6. 85,642
11. 1792
13. 50,540
15. 900

60. MATHOSAURUS: WHAT WAS I? Iguanodon

61. WHAT HAS SHARP TEETH, CHOPS DOWN CHERRY TREES, AND NEVER TELLS LIES? Jaws Washington

62. WHAT KIND OF GUM DO WHALES CHEW? Blubber gum

63. WHAT KIND OF FISH DO KNIGHTS EAT? Swordfish

64. WHAT DID THE BOY SAY WHEN HE OPENED HIS PIGGY BANK AND FOUND NOTHING? O I C U R M T

65. WHAT INVENTION ALLOWS YOU TO SEE THROUGH WALLS? A window

68. SHARED SIDES

9	18	6	13
16	3	18	7
4	14	2	17
9	5	15	8

2 3 4 5 6 7 8 9

8	18	7	11
13	3	19	4
2	16	5	18
8	6	20	9

2 3 4 5 6 7 8 9

69. MATH MAZE

6	2	1	8	4	7
8	6	4	2	1	2
1	3	3	2	5	3
7	9	2	6	4	1

192

1	2	3	5	3	4
4	1	6	2	2	3
3	6	2	9	6	1
7	4	5	1	8	5
5	8	2	4	3	1
2	1	9	3	5	7

192

1	2	3	5	3	4
4	1	6	2	2	3
3	6	2	9	6	1
7	4	5	1	8	5
5	8	2	4	3	1
2	1	9	3	5	7

360

70. OPERATIONAL CHOICES

2 x 4 + 3 = 11
x + - +
6 + 3 x 2 = 18
- - x -
5 + 4 x 1 = 9
= = = =
7 x 3 - 1 = 20

71. USING WHOLE NUMBERS WITH GEOMETRY

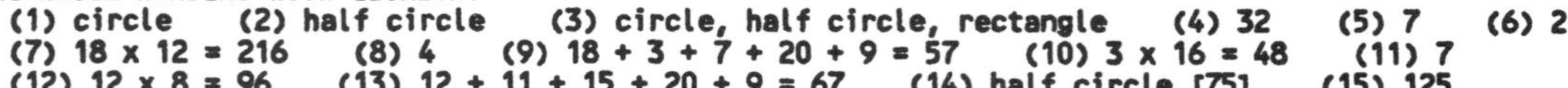

(1) circle (2) half circle (3) circle, half circle, rectangle (4) 32 (5) 7 (6) 2
(7) 18 x 12 = 216 (8) 4 (9) 18 + 3 + 7 + 20 + 9 = 57 (10) 3 x 16 = 48 (11) 7
(12) 12 x 8 = 96 (13) 12 + 11 + 15 + 20 + 9 = 67 (14) half circle [75] (15) 125

72. FILL IN THE MISSING DIGITS

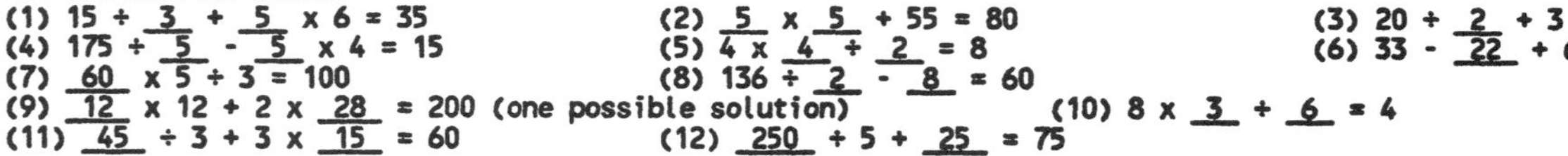

(1) 15 ÷ 3 + 5 x 6 = 35
(2) 5 x 5 + 55 = 80
(3) 20 ÷ 2 + 3 x 6 = 28
(4) 175 ÷ 5 - 5 x 4 = 15
(5) 4 x 4 ÷ 2 = 8
(6) 33 - 22 + 64 ÷ 8 = 19
(7) 60 x 5 ÷ 3 = 100
(8) 136 ÷ 2 - 8 = 60
(9) 12 x 12 + 2 x 28 = 200 (one possible solution)
(10) 8 x 3 ÷ 6 = 4
(11) 45 ÷ 3 + 3 x 15 = 60
(12) 250 ÷ 5 + 25 = 75

73. "30" MATH

(1) 9 x 3 = 27 + 8 = 35 - 5 = 30
(2) 4 x 6 = 24 + 3 = 27 + 3 = 30
(3) 9 x 6 = 54 ÷ 2 = 27 + 3 = 30
(4) 7 x 6 = 42 - 4 = 38 - 8 = 30
(5) 9 x 5 = 45 ÷ 3 = 15 x 2 = 30
(6) 8 x 8 = 64 ÷ 2 = 32 - 2 = 30

74. BOX EQUATIONS

8 x 2 - 2 = 14
\+   +   +   +
5 + 6 - 1 = 10
\-   ÷   +   -
4 + 4 + 3 = 11
=   =   =   =
9 - 2 + 6 = 13

75. PUZZLERS

(1) 6 x 6 + 6 = 42
(2) $\frac{4}{4} + 4 \times 4 = 17$
(3) $\frac{55}{55} + 5 = 6$
(4) $7 \times 7 \times \frac{7}{7} = 49$
(5) 23 x 2 + 2 + 2 = 50
(6) 11 + 11 + 11 x 1 x 1 = 33
(7) 6 x 2 x 2 + 26 = 50
(8) $\frac{1}{1} + \frac{1}{1} + \frac{1}{1} + \frac{1}{1} + \frac{1}{1} = 5$
(9) 22 x 2 x 2 = 88
(10) 31 x 1 + 3 + 1 = 35

76. SCHOOL LUNCH MENU

EGGS:

20	6		40	3		
10)200	x20	120 eggs or 10 doz.	5)200	x40	120 eggs or 10 doz.	TOTAL: 20 doz.
120			120			

FLOUR:	2	3	40 cups	
	x20	x40	+120 cups	TOTAL: 160 cups
	40	120	160	
BUTTER:	1	1	20 cups	
	x20	x40	+40 cups	TOTAL: 60 cups
	20	40	60	
MILK:	1	2	20 cups	
	x20	x40	+80 cups	TOTAL: 100 cups
	20	80	100	
SALT:	2	1	40 tsp.	
	x20	x40	+40 tsp.	TOTAL: 80 tsp.
	40	40	80	

77. FIND THE SUM

cone - 31 + 19 + 15 + 13 + 1 = 79
donuts - 18 + 17 + 19 + 9 = 63
tree - 14 + 9 + 29 + 34 = 86
flowers - 45 + 33 + 19 + 8 + 11 = 116

78. SHAPE MATH

(1)		(2)		(3)		(4)		(5)	
= 3	3235	= 2	25	= 5	56	= 2	2222	= 5	15 / 5)75
= 5	155	= 5	x 5	= 6	x 6	= 1	+1011	= 7	5
= 1	133	= 1	125	= 3	336	= 0	3233	= 1	25
= 2	3523					= 3		= 2	25

79. MATH SQUARES

3 SQUARE

40	5	30
15	25	35
20	45	10

4 SQUARE

31	3	5	25
9	21	19	15
17	13	11	23
7	27	29	1

80. OPERATION SOLUTIONS

(1) 9 + 7 x 3 = 30
(2) 12 ÷ 4 + 5 + 6 ÷ 3 = 10
(3) 6 + 42 - 32 = 16
(4) 10 + 20 ÷ 5 x 4 = 26
(5) 105 ÷ 5 x 2 + 25 = 67
(6) 16 ÷ 8 + 42 - 12 = 32
(7) 8 - 6 + 24 - 4 + 2 = 24
(8) 42 - 4 + 1 - 24 = 15
(9) 3 + 21 + 3 - 21 = 6
(10) 12 - 64 ÷ 32 = 10
(11) 24 x 12 ÷ 6 ÷ 3 - 2 - 1 = 13
(12) 9 - 3 + 6 - 2 + 31 = 41

81. CIRCULAR MATH

It works because the computations end up canceling themselves out - in other words, the operations and numbers equal zero, so you end up with your original number!

82. MATH PATTERNS

(1) Add odd numbers (1, 3, 5, 7, 9, etc.)
1, 2, 5, 10, 17, 26, 37, 50
+3 +5 +7 +9 +11 +13

(2) Add each consecutive number
2 + 2 = 4 + 2 = 6 + 10 = 16
2, 2, 4, 6, 10, 16, 26, 42, 68

(3) Add 1 then 2 then 3, etc.
1 + 1 = 2 + 2 = 4 + 3 = 7 + 4 = 11, etc.
1, 2, 4, 7, 11, 16, 22, 29
+5 +6 +7

(4) 52, 47, 42, 37, 32, 27, 22
Alternate numbers and subtract 10 from each.

52	47	42	37	32
-10	-10	-10	-10	-10
42	37	32	27	22

(5) Add prime numbers (1, 2, 3, 5, 7, etc.)
1, 2, 4, 7, 12, 19, 30, 43, 50
+11 +13 +17

(6) Add even numbers
1 + 2 = 3 + 4 = 7 + 6 = 13 + 8 = 21
1, 3, 7, 13, 21, 31, 43, 57

(7) Every other number add 1 (1, 2, 3, 4)
Every other number subtract 2 (43, 41, 39)
1, 43, 2, 41, 3, 39, 4, 37, 5, 35, 6

(8) 1 x 1 = 2
2 x 2 = 4
3 x 3 = 9
4 x 4 = 16
5 x 5 = 25
6 x 6 = 36
7 x 7 = 49
8 x 8 = 64

2, 4, 9, 16, 25, 36, 49, 64

(9) Each number multiplied by 2, then 3, then 4, then 5, etc.

11	22	66	264	1,320	7,920	50,440
x 2	x 3	x 4	x 5	x 6	x 7	x 8
22	66	264	1320	7,920	55,440	443,520

11, 22, 66, 264, 1320, 7,920, 55,440, 443,520

(10) Every other number add 3
Every other number add 5
3, 5, 6, 10, 9, 15, 12, 20, 15, 25

83. HOW MANY WAYS CAN YOU MAKE CHANGE?

	5	10	25	50
1.	20			
2.	18	1		
3.	16	2		
4.	15		1	
5.	14	3		
6.	13	1	1	
7.	12	4		
8.	11	2	1	
9.	10	5		
10.	10		2	
11.	10			1
12.	9	3	1	
13.	8	6		
14.	8	1	2	
15.	8	1		1
16.	7	4	1	
17.	6	7		
18.	6	2	2	
19.	6	2		1
20.	5		3	

	5	10	25	50
21.	5		1	1
22.	5	5	1	
23.	4	8		
24.	4	3	2	
25.	4	3		1
26.	3	6	1	
27.	3	1	3	
28.	3	1	1	1
29.	2	9		
30.	2	4	2	
31.	2	4		1
32.	1	2	3	
33.	1	2	1	1
34.	1	7	1	
35.		10		
36.		5	2	
37.		5		1
38.			4	
39.			2	1
40.				2

84. HONEYCOMB MATH

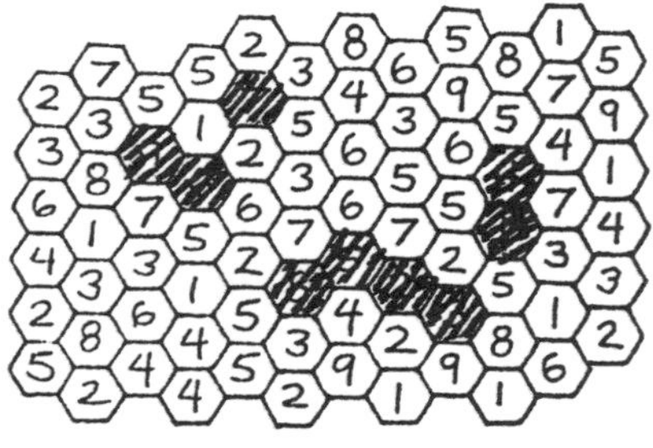

85. LETTER CODE

H	o	s	p	i	t	a	b	l	e
0	1	2	3	4	5	6	7	8	9

```
   129        689       86       51
3)387     4)2756    4)344    4)204      359      9895
  300       2400      320      20      -295     - 359
   87        356       24       4        64      9536
   60        320       24       4
   27         36
   27         36
```

86. MULTIPLICATION STUMPERS

(1) 1-1/2 men + 1-1/2 men = 3 men
1-1/2 boats + 1-1/2 boats = 3 boats > so 3 men build 3 boats in 1-1/2 days
So:
7 men build 7 boats in 1-1/2 days
7 men build 14 boats in 3 days
7 men build 28 boats in 6 days [28 boats]

(2) $\frac{4 \times 3}{2} = 6$

(3) 3 possibilities:
B Br
Br Br
B B

(4) 10

10 1st day
14 2nd day
18 3rd day
22 4th day
+26 5th day
90